Stephanie

Heldoms

FUTURE GRACE
DVD STUDY GUIDE

D1615995

A 12-part study of FUTURE GRACE
by JOHN PIPER

FUTURE GRACE
DVD STUDY GUIDE

The Purifying Power of the Promises of God

MULTNOMAH
BOOKS

FUTURE GRACE DVD STUDY GUIDE
PUBLISHED BY MULTNOMAH BOOKS
12265 Oracle Boulevard, Suite 200
Colorado Springs, Colorado 80921

ISBN 978-1-60142-434-1

Published in the United States by WaterBrook Multnomah, an imprint of the Crown Publishing Group, a division of Random House Inc., New York.

MULTNOMAH and its mountain colophon are registered trademarks of Random House Inc.

Printed in the United States of America
2012—First Edition

10 9 8 7 6 5 4 3 2 1

SPECIAL SALES
Most WaterBrook Multnomah books are available at special quantity discounts when purchased in bulk by corporations, organizations, and special-interest groups. Custom imprinting or excerpting can also be done to fit special needs. For information, please e-mail SpecialMarkets@WaterBrookMultnomah.com or call 1-800-603-7051.

CONTENTS

INTRODUCTION TO
THIS STUDY GUIDE

F aith. Grace. Obedience. Gratitude. Cross. Promises. Warnings. Holy Spirit. Justification. Sanctification. All of these play a role in living the Christian life. All Christians know that we should believe in Jesus and his sacrificial death. All Christians also know that we should obey Jesus in the present. And all Christians know that God has made very great promises to us for the future. But even this short summary raises a number of challenging and very important questions. For instance:

- How can something that happened two thousand years ago empower me to live obediently in the present?
- What do Christians mean by "faith," and what is the object of our faith?
- Is grace pardon from sin or power over sin?
- What is justification? How does it relate to sanctification?
- Where does power for present obedience come from?
- Should we obey God in an effort to pay him back for all the good that he has done for us?
- Should we live the Christian life by faith or by the power of the Holy Spirit?
- And how do the answers to all of these questions actually work in everyday life? How does faith, grace, gratitude, etc., actually enable us to overcome anxiety, covetousness, lust, and impatience?
- In short, what does it mean to *actually live* the Christian life?

The aim of this study guide is to aid you as you to seek to unravel the practical mysteries of the Christian life. Our hope is that as you work through this DVD and study guide, you would grow in your understanding of the dynamics of the Christian life, the particular ways that the faith relates to the past, the present, and the future, and the way that God by his grace and through the Holy Spirit equips you with everything you need to do his will. More than that, our prayer is that you would not merely *understand* how to live the Christian life, but that you would be empowered by the grace of God to resist the fleeting pleasures of sin, to put to death the various sins and struggles that so easily entangle, and to embrace all that God is for you in Christ.

This study guide is designed for a twelve-session,[1] guided group study that focuses on the *Future Grace* DVD Set.[2] After an introductory lesson, each subsequent lesson examines one 25-minute session[3] from *Future Grace.* You are encouraged to prepare for the viewing of each session by reading and reflecting upon Scripture, by considering key quotations, and by asking yourself penetrating questions. Your preparatory work for each lesson is marked with the heading "Before You Watch the DVD, Study and Prepare" in Lessons 2–11.

The workload is conveniently divided into five daily, manageable assignments. There is also a section suggesting further study. This work is to be completed individually before the group convenes to view the DVD and discuss the material.

Throughout this study guide, paragraphs printed in this typeface are excerpts from a book written by John Piper (or occasionally another author) or excerpts taken from the Desiring God website (www.desiringgod.org). They are included to supplement the study questions and to summarize key or provocative points.

The second section in Lessons 2–11, titled "Further Up and Further In," is designed for the learner who wants to explore the concepts and ideas introduced in the lesson in greater detail. This section is not required, but it will deepen your understanding of the material.

The third section in Lessons 2–11, titled "While You Watch the

DVD, Take Notes," is to be completed as the DVD is playing. This section includes fill-in-the-blanks and leaves space for note taking. You are encouraged to engage with the DVD by filling in the appropriate blanks and writing down other notes that will aid you in the group discussion.

The fourth section in each normal lesson is "After You Watch the DVD, Discuss What You've Learned." Three discussion questions are provided to guide and focus the conversation. You may record, in the spaces provided, notes that will help you contribute to the conversation. Or you may use this space to record things from the discussion that you want to remember.

The final section is an application section: "After You Discuss, Make Application." You will be challenged to record a "takeaway point" and to engage in a certain activity that is a fitting response to the content presented in the lesson.

Group leaders will want to review the Leader's Guide, included at the end of this study guide, immediately.

Life transformation will only occur by the grace of God. Therefore, we highly encourage you to seek the Lord in prayer throughout the learning process. Pray that God would open your eyes to see wonderful things in his Word. Pray that he would grant you the insight and concentration you need in order to get the most from this resource. Pray that God would cause you to not merely understand the truth but also to rejoice in it. And pray that the discussion in your group would be mutually encouraging and edifying. We've included objectives at the beginning of each lesson. These objectives won't be realized without the gracious work of God through prayer.

INTRODUCTION TO
FUTURE GRACE

A Companion Study to the Future Grace *DVD, Session 1*

LESSON OBJECTIVES

It is our prayer that after you have finished this lesson...

- You will get a feel for how you and others in your group approach the issue of sanctification and the Christian life.
- Your curiosity would be roused, and questions would begin to come to mind.
- You will be eager to learn more about what it means to live by faith in future grace.

ABOUT YOURSELF

1. What is your name?

2. Tell the group something about yourself that they probably don't already know.

3. What are you hoping to learn from this group study?

→» *While You Watch the DVD, Take Notes* «←

What struggle shaped John Piper as a boy? *fearful - couldn't speck in*
he's after help in the Bible   *Front of people*

This is a seminar on ___*sanctification- we through & the spirit are being transferred*___
                                    justification- Jesus did firus

This is a seminar on ___*Future Grace*___.
                          press on, reach out because I have been
This is a seminar on - ___*Always His own*___.
                          made his

This is a seminar on ___*Glory of God*___.
                    Fearlessness & hope
                    The Gospel

COURSE OUTLINE

1. *Definitions*
   We get God & nothing else will suffice
2. *Standing on the promises of God*
   why does it matter
3. *Is it Biblical*
4. *How does it work* *for holiness*
5. *How does it work against sin.*

→ *After You Watch the DVD, Discuss What You've Learned* ←

1. In what ways has your background shaped your theology? Are there any particular struggles in your life that have left a deep impression on your thinking?

2. Discuss Philippians 3:8–16. What does John Piper mean by "I reach out because I've been reached" and how is that statement supported in this passage?

   Pressing on, God holds onto us.
   Even when I don't feel passionate about God - press on

3. Based on the course outline, what part of the course are you most eager to explore? Why?

→ *After You Discuss, Make Application* ←

1. What was the most meaningful part of this lesson for you? Was there a sentence, concept, or idea that really struck you? Why? Record your thoughts in the space below.

   He made me his own

2. In the DVD session, John Piper mentioned the hymn "Standing on the Promises of God" by R. Kelso Carter. The lyrics to this hymn are provided below. Use these lyrics during your devotional time this week as a way of preparing your heart and mind for the rest of this study.

Standing on the promises of Christ my King,
Through eternal ages let His praises ring,
Glory in the highest, I will shout and sing,
Standing on the promises of God.

Refrain
Standing, standing,
Standing on the promises of God my Savior;
Standing, standing,
I'm standing on the promises of God.

Standing on the promises that cannot fail,
When the howling storms of doubt and fear assail,
By the living Word of God I shall prevail,
Standing on the promises of God.

Standing on the promises I now can see
Perfect, present cleansing in the blood for me;
Standing in the liberty where Christ makes free,
Standing on the promises of God.

Standing on the promises of Christ the Lord,
Bound to Him eternally by love's strong cord,
Overcoming daily with the Spirit's sword,
Standing on the promises of God.

Standing on the promises I cannot fall,
Listening every moment to the Spirit's call
Resting in my Savior as my all in all,
Standing on the promises of God.

DEFINING OUR TERMS

A Companion Study to the Future Grace *DVD, Session 2*

LESSON OBJECTIVES

It is our prayer that after you have finished this lesson...
- You will have a better understanding of the meaning of "past," "present," and "future" in this study.
- You will develop initial definitions of faith and grace to aid you as we begin this study.
- You will identify some of the key passions that undergird this study.

→* *Before You Watch the DVD, Study and Prepare* *←

DAY 1—DEFINING TIME

Time is one of the most prevalent and elusive concepts in the world. All of us live in time, make use of time, and talk about time, but precisely defining the nature of time has proven challenging to even the best philosophers and theologians. Given that the focus of this study is on *future* grace, it is important that we at least have some common understanding of what we mean by "future" (as well as "past" and "present").

* **Question 1:** Give a basic definition of "past," "present," and "future." There's no need to be overly philosophical. Focus on what you think most people mean by these terms in everyday conversation.

> *Past = before right now*
> *Present = right now*
> *future = what will happen*

This is a study on *future* grace. However, throughout the lessons we will also be discussing past and present grace. As we think about these realities, it is important that they not be abstract and distant, but concrete and personal.

Question 2: Reflect on your own life and write down some examples of past, present, and future grace. They can be big and meaningful examples of grace, or small and relatively insignificant examples of grace.

> *Moving to WA - provision of house, friends*
> *miscarriages = health*
> *Corran after m/c*

Day 2—Preliminary Definitions

In order to begin our study, we will also need to have some working definitions of other key terms. Later in the study, we will refine and clarify our definitions based on the Scriptures. For now, focus on what you believe certain key biblical terms mean.

* **Question 3:** Define faith. Cite Scripture in your answer. You may also note definitions that you've heard from other people.

> *being certain of what you cannot see*
> *Heb 11:1 Now faith is being sure of what we hope for & certain of what we do not see*

Question 4: Define grace. Cite Scripture in your answer. You may also note definitions that you've heard from other people.

Grace - getting something (good) we don't deserve / didn't earn

Eph 2:8 For it is by Grace you have been saved, through Faith - and this is not from ourselves, it is the gift of God

DAY 3—INITIAL EXAMPLES OF LIVING BY FAITH IN FUTURE GRACE

Examine Hebrews 11:1 and 11:6.

Now faith is the assurance of things hoped for, the conviction of things not seen.

And without faith it is impossible to please him, for whoever would draw near to God must believe that he exists and that he rewards those who seek him.

* **Question 5:** Underline every reference to faith (or every parallel to faith) in this passage. Then circle every reference to something future.

Reflect on 1 Peter 4:11.

Whoever speaks, as one who speaks oracles of God; whoever serves, as one who serves by the strength that God supplies— in order that in everything God may be glorified through Jesus Christ. To him belong glory and dominion forever and ever. Amen.

Question 6: According to this passage, how should we serve others? What is the purpose of our serving in this way? Give an example of a time when you've sought to apply this verse in your own life.

So that it brings glory to God

DAY 4—INTRODUCING THE DEBTOR'S ETHIC

The debtor's ethic is one of the key reasons that John Piper initially wrote the book *Future Grace*. This concept will be explored more fully in Lesson 8. For now, we will simply focus on the use of the term *debtor* in a key passage of Scripture.

Read Romans 8:12–13.

[12] So then, brothers, we are debtors, not to the flesh, to live according to the flesh. [13] For if you live according to the flesh you will die, but if by the Spirit you put to death the deeds of the body, you will live.

Question 7: Notice that Paul says we are debtors, but he doesn't say to whom. If you were going to finish Paul's statement in verse 12, how would you do it? To whom are Christians debtors? Why do you think Paul doesn't finish that statement?

* **Question 8:** Some Christians say that we should seek to pay God back for all of the good that he has done for us. Where can you find this idea in the Bible? If you were going to try and pay God back, what would you do?   *fail*

DAY 5—WHY DOES IT MATTER?

If you're familiar with the ministry of John Piper, you know that there are some foundational passions underneath everything that he writes and says.

Let your passion be single—it wasn't always easy for me to love this topic because I couldn't make my passions single. I knew from growing up in my father's house that one passion was unavoidable and centrally biblical, and that was a passion for the glory of God. My father quoted as often as any other text, "Johnny, whatever you do, whether you eat or whether you drink, do everything to the glory of God" (1 Corinthians 10:31). So, I grew up knowing that was one passion that had to be there.… Well, that was one. Now here I am a teenager, knowing, perhaps not as clearly from Scripture, but from my own soul, that I had another passion. I wanted to be happy.… Call it what you will: joy, satisfaction, contentment. It doesn't matter, they are all in the Bible. The Bible is indiscriminate in its pleasure language.[4]

Question 9: What are the two great passions of John Piper's life? Where would you go in Scripture to find these passions?

For the glory of God
happiness

I only have one thing to say.... I sum it up in little words like this: "God is most glorified in me when I am most satisfied in him."

These are not two projects. These are not two passions. These are one passion. To know him with the mind and delight in what you know of him in the heart is one passion. God is glorified by being delighted *in.*

* **Question 10:** How do you think the subject of this study, living by faith in future grace, relates to these foundational passions?

FURTHER UP AND FURTHER IN

Note: The "Further Up and Further In" section is for those who want to study more. It is a section for further reference and going deeper. The phrase "further up and further in" is borrowed from C. S. Lewis.

Read or listen to "Let Your Passion Be Single," an online sermon at the Desiring God website.

Question 11: We've already seen the two passions that John Piper felt in his early years. Why did he feel the tension between them?

Question 12: What did John Piper learn from (1) Blaise Pascal, (2) C. S. Lewis, and (3) Jonathan Edwards that helped him to resolve the tension between a passion for God's glory and a passion for happiness?

Question 13: Which objection to Christian Hedonism do you think is the strongest? In your mind, does John Piper respond to each objection adequately?

Read or listen to "The Faith of Noah, Abraham, and Sarah," an online sermon at the Desiring God website.

Question 14: According to John Piper, why is the faith in Hebrews 11 not an add-on to saving faith? What evidence from the context does he present?

Question 15: What are the four elements that are always true of biblical faith? Give an example of each from Hebrews 11:7–12.

[handwritten top margin: trust God for the strengh He supplies 1 Peter 4:11]

[handwritten left margin top: Faith Heb 1:1   11:8,10]

[handwritten left margin vertical: Reliance on Grace — Can't pay back = bottomless line of credit]

→ *While You Watch the DVD, Take Notes* ←

How does John Piper distinguish between past, present, and future?

future - right this second a dot
present - instance of existence almost non-existent nanosecond?
past - resivoir that getting bigger every second

John Piper's definition of grace:

All the good that comes to me
Gods commitment to do only what is good for his unworthy people fulfilling all the promises to them because of Christ

John Piper's definition of faith:

receiving Christ as the supremely valuable treasure that He is.

The secret I am trying to solve is __*why justified faith*__ .
sanctifies

According to John Piper, why won't the debtor's ethic work?

"why do you call me Lord Lord & do not do what I say?"
owe God? Pay Him back? Debtor to Grace
every step I take → deeper in depth. You will never be less in debt today

→ *After You Watch the DVD, Discuss What You've Learned* ←

1. Reflect on John Piper's discussion of past, present, and future.
   Did you find his comments helpful? Discuss the differences
   between past grace and future grace.

[handwritten bottom margin: Is 48:9 "I do it for my own sake"]

2. Discuss John Piper's definitions of faith, grace, and bygone grace. Do these definitions seem biblical? What disagreements, additions, or clarifications do you have related to his definitions?

We are not able to love God w/ all heart
God gave us Christ to help us.
Constant provision -

3. Have you ever used the debtor's ethic to motivate obedience? Discuss Piper's objections to it. What remaining questions do you have about the debtor's ethic?

→* *After You Discuss, Make Application* *←

1. What was the most meaningful part of this lesson for you? Was there a sentence, concept, or idea that really struck you? Why? Record your thoughts in the space below.

2. Make a list of future situations, needs, or concerns in your life. Begin to pray regularly for these future items on your list by asking God to give you faith in the present that his grace will be there for you in the future. Refer back to this list as you progress through this study.

1) Passion for the Supremacy of God

2# A Passion for Joy   Ps 100:2
       not reluctant   2 Cor 9:7

   Living by faith in future grace means
   rejoicing in future grace

A PASSION FOR HOLINESS

A Companion Study to the Future Grace *DVD, Session 3*

LESSON OBJECTIVES

It is our prayer that after you have finished this lesson…
- You will embrace the importance of practical holiness.
- You will recognize the necessity of holiness and perseverance for final salvation.
- You will have a clearer understanding of the relationship between eternal security and the necessity of holiness.

→ *Before You Watch the DVD, Study and Prepare* ←

DAY 1—DEFINING HOLINESS

Once again, it's important that we carefully define our terms so as to prevent confusion and misunderstanding.

* **Question 1:** Define holiness. Cite Scripture in your answer. What does it mean for a person to be holy? Give some examples of practical holiness, either from the Bible or from your own life.

Ps 99:9 for the Lord our God is Holy

Heb 12:10 God disciplines us for our good, that we may share in his holiness

:14 without holiness no one will see the Lord

Read 1 Thessalonians 3:11–13.

is holiness

[11]Now may our God and Father himself, and our Lord Jesus, direct our way to you, [12]and may the Lord make you increase and abound in love for one another and for all, as we do for you, [13]so that he may establish your hearts blameless in holiness before our God and Father, at the coming of our Lord Jesus with all his saints.

Question 2: According to these verses, what is the relationship between holiness and love?

The Lord makes us increase in love & abound in love for eachother, so that he may establish our hearts blameless in holiness before God

Sanctification is the process of becoming holy. And what Paul has in mind by holiness was already signaled back in 3:12–13, just 4 verses earlier. "May the Lord make you increase and *abound in love* to one another and to all men, as we do to you, so that he may establish your hearts unblamable in *holiness* before our God." If abounding in *love* is the means by which our hearts are established in *holiness,* then love must be the thing Paul has in mind when he exhorts us to make progress in holiness or sanctification.[5]

DAY 2—NO HOLINESS, NO HEAVEN

One of the central teachings of the Bible is that justification is by faith alone (Romans 3:28; 5:1). Salvation is by grace through faith, and not of works (Ephesians 2:8–9). Paul celebrates the fact that the free gift of God is eternal life in Christ Jesus (Romans 6:23) and that nothing can separate us from the love of God in Christ (Romans 8:39). But the Bible also contains provocative language about the necessity of holiness.

Meditate on Hebrews 12:14; Galatians 6:7–9; and 1 John 2:4.

Strive for peace with everyone, and for the holiness without which no one will see the Lord.

⁷Do not be deceived: God is not mocked, for whatever one sows, that will he also reap. ⁸For the one who sows to his own flesh will from the flesh reap corruption, but the one who sows to the Spirit will from the Spirit reap eternal life. ⁹And let us not grow weary of doing good, for in due season we will reap, if we do not give up.

Whoever says "I know him" but does not keep his commandments is a liar, and the truth is not in him.

Question 3: Summarize the teaching of these passages in your own words. What is at stake in our pursuit of holiness?

> remain peaceful
> the things we do/what we sow.
> Hypocrites saying you know Jesus but not keeping commandments

Now we begin to see what is going on in this church. Evidently there was a group who knew about the doctrine of justification by faith. It's the doctrine that Paul emphasized in Romans and Galatians. It said that through faith in Christ we can be acquitted of all our sins and can stand righteous before God on account of the death of Christ.

But there were many in the early church who took Paul's doctrine and distorted it to teach things that Paul rejected. Some said, "Let us do evil that good may come" (Romans 3:8). Some said, "Let us sin that grace may abound" (Romans 6:1). And Paul corrected both of these abuses of the doctrine in the book of Romans.

Some said that faith can justify a person whether that faith gives rise to good works or not. And James responds in the second chapter of his letter, "What does it profit, my brethren, if a man says he has faith but has not works? Can his faith save him?" And others said—these are the false prophets behind first John—"You can be righteous even if you don't do righteousness." To which John responds with this powerful letter, and especially 3:7, "Let no one deceive you: he who does righteousness is righteous." What you do is a test of what you are.[6]

* **Question 4:** How would you relate the teaching in the previous question to passages about salvation by grace and through faith? For example, how can eternal life be a free gift (Romans 6:23) and the result of sowing to the Spirit (Galatians 6:8)?

DAY 3—LOSS OF SALVATION OR LOSS OF REWARDS?

Christians often disagree about the proper understanding of the passages in the previous questions (and others like them). Some Christians argue that such passages teach that Christians can lose their salvation through persistent and willful sin. Other Christians argue that such passages threaten loss of rewards in heaven, but that Christians will go to heaven regardless of how they live their lives.

* **Question 5:** Interact with the following position: "Passages like Hebrews 12:14; 1 John 2:4; and other warning passages teach that it is possible for Christians to lose their salvation through persistent and willful sin. Genuine Christians can sin too much and thus lose the salvation they formerly possessed, resulting in their punishment in hell."

> *I don't agree these passages are talking about genuine Christians*

Question 6: Interact with the following position: "Warning passages in the Bible should be understood as threatening genuine Christians with loss of reward in heaven. Once a person is saved, they will always be saved, regardless of whether they walk in obedience to God. Those who believe in Jesus will go to heaven no matter how they live their lives. Even if they turn away from the faith completely, God will still save them based on their initial act of faith."

> *Parable of lost sheep that wandered away - Jesus pursues that lamb. I believe he will pursue a wanderer who had been genuine in being born again*

DAY 4—WHAT WOULD YOU SAY?

Imagine the following scenario (if you're a woman, reverse the sexes so that the adulterous spouse is a woman):

> Harry has been a professing believer since he was in college. He is now in his midforties. He and his family are

members of your church, but they are not heavily involved. Over the past year, Harry has become sexually
involved with a woman who is not his wife. This adulterous affair has now been exposed. Harry has been con-
fronted by his close friend Jim, but has rejected Jim's pleas
to repent and return to his wife. Jim has now asked that
you go with him to meet again with Harry.

* **Question 7:** What would you say to Harry?

Wherever come home, your not too far,
A true believer does not continue to sin
God always provides a way out.

Question 8: How do you know that you will wake up believing
in Jesus tomorrow? What gives you confidence that you won't
wake up and reject Christ?

Its a daily disciple to follow him e
not wander off. I'm on the outskirts of his fold
when I'm not in regular study - much
Picture of Corren in seattle - need to me us more likely
ahead to wander too far

DAY 5—THE PROMISE OF PERSEVERANCE

Thus far in this lesson we've focused on the necessity of our perseverance
and different views of the consequences of failure to persevere. In this
final day, we will look at promises of God related to our perseverance.

Meditate on Philippians 1:6 and 1 Corinthians 1:4–9.

And I am sure of this, that he who began a good work in you will
bring it to completion at the day of Jesus Christ.

[4]I give thanks to my God always for you because of the grace of
God that was given you in Christ Jesus, [5]that in every way you
were enriched in him in all speech and all knowledge—[6]even as

the testimony about Christ was confirmed among you—[7]so that you are not lacking in any spiritual gift, as you wait for the revealing of our Lord Jesus Christ, [8]who will sustain you to the end, guiltless in the day of our Lord Jesus Christ. [9]God is faithful, by whom you were called into the fellowship of his Son, Jesus Christ our Lord.

* **Question 9:** What is the basis of Paul's confidence that the Philippians and Corinthians will persevere to the end? Underline the relevant statements.

Reflect on Hebrews 13:20–21.

[20]Now may the God of peace who brought again from the dead our Lord Jesus, the great shepherd of the sheep, by the blood of the eternal covenant, [21]equip you with everything good that you may do his will, working in us that which is pleasing in his sight, through Jesus Christ, to whom be glory forever and ever. Amen.

Question 10: What is the heart of the author's request to God on behalf of his readers? How will they be equipped to do the will of God? Underline the relevant phrase.

FURTHER UP AND FURTHER IN

Read "Letter to a Friend Concerning the So-Called 'Lordship Salvation,'" an online article at the Desiring God website.

Question 11: What does Piper mean by the two-stage, Savior-Lord paradigm of salvation? Have you ever encountered this paradigm?

"Submitting to the lordship of Christ is a lifelong activity. It must be renewed every day in many ~~texts~~ acts of trust and obedience. Submission to Christ's lordship is not merely a once for all

Question 12: What is Piper's central biblical problem with the ~~typical~~ two-stage model of salvation? What alternative does he put forth?

Question 13: How does Piper establish that Lordship Salvation is nothing other than salvation by faith?

Question 14: How would Piper preach to disobedient, professing Christians? What is your assessment of his approach? Do you believe that it is biblical?

"A person that goes on willfully rejecting the commands of Jesus for his life have no warrant for salvation

Question 15: Which arguments did you find the most compelling? Which biblical texts were most helpful? What remaining questions do you have about this issue?

Jn 14:15 If you love me you will keep my commands

Jn 3:16

Rom 6:12

1Jn 2:4

⟶ *While You Watch the DVD, Take Notes* ⟵

What does John Piper mean by practical holiness?

Obedience to Gods word in egdy life

Gal 6:8-9 - Romas 8:30 the us is the who don't grow wary in dois good

No _holiness_, No _heaven_

The _____ required _____ us will be_____ us.

Eternal security is not _automatic_.

How does John Piper know that he'll wake up a Christian?

He puts the fear of Him in your hart Jer. Our perseverance is a work of God, because the power of God will keep me in the faith

Does John Piper believe that people can lose their salvation?

⟶ *After You Watch the DVD, Discuss What You've Learned* ⟵

1. Discuss any remaining questions you have about the necessity of perseverance for final salvation. Were you persuaded by the arguments presented in this lesson?

2. In your own words, resolve the tension between the Bible's teaching on eternal security and the Bible's teaching on the necessity of perseverance. What modifications, additions, or clarifications would you make to Piper's understanding of these issues?

3. How would you confront a professing believer who is living in persistent sin?

→❋ *After You Discuss, Make Application* ❋←

1. What was the most meaningful part of this lesson for you? Was there a sentence, concept, or idea that really struck you? Why? Record your thoughts in the space below.

2. Memorize Jeremiah 32:40 or Hebrews 13:20–21.

JUSTIFICATION BY FAITH AND THE NECESSITY OF PERSEVERANCE

A Companion Study to the Future Grace *DVD, Session 4*

LESSON OBJECTIVES

It is our prayer that after you have finished this lesson...

- You will have a better understanding of the ground, means, and evidence of salvation.
- You will begin to explore the connection between the work of the Holy Spirit in sanctification and our faith.
- You will be practically helped in your fight to resist temptation through a clearer picture of our ultimate reward.

→* *Before You Watch the DVD, Study and Prepare* *←

DAY 1—JUSTIFICATION BY FAITH ALONE

One of the most precious truths in the Bible is the doctrine of justification by faith alone. Here is a summary of this doctrine from the

Bethlehem Baptist Church Elder Affirmation of Faith, Section 9, available at hopeingod.org:

> 9.1 We believe that in a free act of righteous grace God justifies the ungodly by faith alone apart from works, pardoning their sins, and reckoning them as righteous and acceptable in His presence. Faith is thus the sole instrument by which we, as sinners, are united to Christ, whose perfect righteousness and satisfaction for sins is alone the ground of our acceptance with God. This acceptance happens fully and permanently at the first instant of justification. Thus the righteousness by which we come into right standing with God is not anything worked in us by God, neither imparted to us at baptism nor over time, but rather is accomplished for us, outside ourselves, and is imputed to us.

* **Question 1:** In your mind what are the most significant aspects of this doctrine? Underline key phrases. When does our acceptance with God happen? What is the ground of our acceptance? What is the instrument or means of our acceptance?

Read Romans 5:1.

> Therefore, since we have been justified by faith, we have peace with God through our Lord Jesus Christ.

Question 2: How would you reconcile Romans 5:1 and the summary of the doctrine of justification above with the necessity of perseverance which we saw in the last lesson?

DAY 2—RESOLVING THE TENSION

During the DVD session, John Piper will make reference to the Westminster Confession of Faith, an important summary of biblical teaching used by many Christian denominations. It will be helpful to look closely at the relevant section before watching the video.

Westminster Confession of Faith, Chapter XI

Section I.—Those whom God effectually calleth, he also freely justifieth: not by infusing righteousness into them, but by pardoning their sins, and by accounting and accepting their persons as righteous; not for anything wrought in them, or done by them, but for Christ's sake alone; not by imputing faith itself, the act of believing, or any other evangelical obedience to them, as their righteousness; but by imputing the obedience and satisfaction of Christ unto them, they receiving and resting on him and his righteousness by faith; which faith they have not of themselves, it is the gift of God.

Section II.—Faith, thus receiving and resting on Christ and his righteousness, is the alone instrument of justification; yet is it not alone in the person justified, but is ever accompanied with all other saving graces, and is no dead faith, but worketh by love.

* **Question 3:** Restate the teaching of this passage in your own words.

If you ask most Christians the question, "*How* does God sanctify us?," you're liable to get one of two answers (at least). Some might say, "God sanctifies us *through the Holy Spirit*." Others might say, "God sanctifies us *through faith*." Both of these answers are biblical (Romans 15:16 and Acts 26:18), but the relationship between these two means may not be clear.

Question 4: How would you relate the work of the Holy Spirit in sanctification to the role of our own faith in sanctification? Be as specific as you can.

Day 3—The Wisdom of Solomon

In seeking to address difficult theological questions (like the relationship between justification by faith and the necessity of perseverance), it is often helpful to make use of analogies in order to illustrate and clarify concepts. One analogy that John Piper will make use of in the video session is drawn from the book of 1 Kings.

Reflect on the story of Solomon and the two prostitutes in 1 Kings 3:16–27.

¹⁶Then two prostitutes came to the king and stood before him. ¹⁷The one woman said, "Oh, my lord, this woman and I live in

the same house, and I gave birth to a child while she was in the house. [18]Then on the third day after I gave birth, this woman also gave birth. And we were alone. There was no one else with us in the house; only we two were in the house. [19]And this woman's son died in the night, because she lay on him. [20]And she arose at midnight and took my son from beside me, while your servant slept, and laid him at her breast, and laid her dead son at my breast. [21]When I rose in the morning to nurse my child, behold, he was dead. But when I looked at him closely in the morning, behold, he was not the child that I had borne." [22]But the other woman said, "No, the living child is mine, and the dead child is yours." The first said, "No, the dead child is yours, and the living child is mine." Thus they spoke before the king.

[23]Then the king said, "The one says, 'This is my son that is alive, and your son is dead'; and the other says, 'No; but your son is dead, and my son is the living one.'" [24]And the king said, "Bring me a sword." So a sword was brought before the king. [25]And the king said, "Divide the living child in two, and give half to the one and half to the other." [26]Then the woman whose son was alive said to the king, because her heart yearned for her son, "Oh, my lord, give her the living child, and by no means put him to death." But the other said, "He shall be neither mine nor yours; divide him." [27]Then the king answered and said, "Give the living child to the first woman, and by no means put him to death; she is his mother."

* **Question 5:** When Solomon gave the command to divide the child in two, what was he looking for? How did the response of the mother help him to make a wise decision?

Question 6: Speculate on how this story might help us understand
the relationship between faith and works, specifically the
biblical teaching on justification by faith and final judgment
according to works.

Day 4—Two Types of Motivation

One of the central questions that we are addressing in this study is the
proper motivation for Christian obedience. Today we will explore two
different ways that God motivates us in Scripture.

Think over Matthew 5:8.

Blessed are the pure in heart, for they shall see God.

* **Question 7:** What is the motive for obedience in this passage?
What type of motivation is it?

Now examine Matthew 5:29–30.

[29] If your right eye causes you to sin, tear it out and throw it away.
For it is better that you lose one of your members than that your
whole body be thrown into hell. [30] And if your right hand causes
you to sin, cut it off and throw it away. For it is better that you
lose one of your members than that your whole body go into hell.

Question 8: What is the motivation for purity in this passage? How does it differ from Matthew 5:8? What type of motivation is this?

Day 5—Motivated by Promise or Warning?

Question 9: When you've experienced temptation in the past, what was a more effective weapon against temptation: promises of future blessing or threats of future punishment? In your experience, is it consistently one or the other? Or does it shift depending on circumstances and temptations? Explain your answer.

The ultimate example of future grace is the hope of heaven. Paul tells us that our sufferings are not worth comparing to the glory that is to be revealed to us (Romans 8:18). He looks to the eternal weight of glory to sustain him in the most difficult trials (2 Corinthians 4:16–18). Therefore, it is worth reflecting on the nature of heaven and the joys that will be present there.

* **Question 10:** When you think about heaven, what comes to mind? What is most attractive to you about heaven? What is least attractive? Does any aspect of heaven concern you or produce fear? Explain your answer.

FURTHER UP AND FURTHER IN

Read the following excerpts from the Bethlehem Baptist Church Elder Affirmation of Faith, Section 10, available at hopeingod.org.

10.2 We believe that the reason justifying faith necessarily sanctifies in this way is fourfold:[7]

First, justifying faith is a persevering, that is, continuing, kind of faith. Even though we are justified at the first instant of saving faith, yet this faith justifies only because it is the kind of faith that will surely persevere. The extension of this faith into the future is, as it were, contained in the first seed of faith, as the oak in the acorn. Thus the moral effects of persevering faith may be rightly described as the effects of justifying faith.

Question 11: Summarize this point in your own words. Unpack the analogy that is used in this passage.

Second, we believe that justifying faith trusts in Christ not only for the gift of imputed righteousness and the forgiveness of sins, but also for the fulfillment of all His promises to us based on that reconciliation. Justifying faith magnifies the finished work of Christ's atonement, by resting securely in all the promises of God obtained and guaranteed by that all-sufficient work.

Question 12: Summarize this point in your own words. How does this point support the notion that justifying faith necessarily sanctifies?

Continue reading the Bethlehem Baptist Church Elder Affirmation of Faith:

> *Third,* we believe that justifying faith embraces Christ in all His roles: Creator, Sustainer, Savior, Teacher, Guide, Comforter, Helper, Friend, Advocate, Protector, and Lord. Justifying faith does not divide Christ, accepting part of Him and rejecting the rest. All of Christ is embraced by justifying faith, even before we are fully aware of, or fully understand, all that He will be for us. As more of Christ is truly revealed to us in His Word, genuine faith recognizes Christ and embraces Him more fully.

> **Question 13:** Restate this section in your own words. How would you respond to someone who said that in her experience, she received Christ only as Savior, and not as Lord (or any of the other roles)?

Read "The Present Power of Heaven and Hell," an online article at the Desiring God website.

> **Question 14:** Choose three of John Piper's points and meditate on the biblical passages he cites. Which of his points surprised you the most?

Read "Can Joy Increase Forever?," an online article at the Desiring God website.

Question 15: Why did John Piper fear heaven as a child? What
insight from Jonathan Edwards rescued him from this fear?
What biblical passage does John Piper cite in support of it?

→ *While You Watch the DVD, Take Notes* ←

What problem is raised by the necessity of holiness?

What is the solution of the Westminster Confession of Faith?

*Faith that justifies is never alone
but is ever accompanied by all
other saving graces*

What is the connection between our faith and the work of the Holy
Spirit in sanctification?

*We receive the H.S.
The faith that justifies is the faith that sanctifies
faith is the agent of works*

What is the point of the analogy of King Solomon and the two
prostitutes for this seminar?

*mom is a done deal, just like I
am born again – done deal
works did not earn her the baby*

What is the central power that sin has over us?

faith sees the root of sin
nobody sins out of duty

sin - keep God be comes more cloudy & harder to see

it makes promise
↓
how defeat? with Superior promises
embrace.
for better future & better satisfaction

How can we practically convince ourselves to resist temptation? *↓*
in heat of moment not best place to fill
tank. Pick time/place & ask God to incline me
to his testimonies.

E 6:13 warnings in the Bible are the flip side of
19:2 future Grace — look what you would miss

After You Watch the DVD, Discuss What You've Learned

1. Clarify the differences between the ground, the means, and the evidence of salvation, according to John Piper.

   Sanctification - refining ourselves.

   Glory of God is man fully alive

2. Discuss John Piper's practical advice on fighting temptation. What was particularly helpful to you in his comments? What counsel would you add?

3. If the way to defeat the satisfaction promised by sin is with the superior satisfaction that comes from God, then it is important to reflect on our vision of heaven and eternal life. When you think about heaven, what comes to your mind? What aspects of John Piper's comments resonated with you?

→ *After You Discuss, Make Application* ←

1. What was the most meaningful part of this lesson for you?
   Was there a sentence, concept, or idea that really struck you?
   Why? Record your thoughts in the space below.

2. This week explain the ground, means, and evidence of salvation to a friend who is not in your group. Be sure to clarify the
   relationships between these three different realities.

- Heldoorns - Bellingham   March 1st 2015
  navigating an interrupted world

Elaine — D. R. healing
  Jonathon - trip march
  Pedro—egas

Amy's mom & niece Emma.

IS IT BIBLICAL?

A Companion Study to the Future Grace *DVD, Session 5*

LESSON OBJECTIVES

It is our prayer that after you have finished this lesson...

- You will recognize the kind of faith that counts before God.
- You will understand the role of the grace of God in sanctification.
- You will be encouraged to appropriate the grace of God for all of your weaknesses.

→* *Before You Watch the DVD, Study and Prepare* *←

DAY 1—WORK OF FAITH

Read 1 Thessalonians 1:2–3 and 2 Thessalonians 1:11–12.

[2]We give thanks to God always for all of you, constantly mentioning you in our prayers, [3]remembering before our God and Father your work of faith and labor of love and steadfastness of hope in our Lord Jesus Christ.

[11]To this end we always pray for you, that our God may make you worthy of his calling and may fulfill every resolve for good and every work of faith by his power, [12]so that the name of our Lord Jesus may be glorified in you, and you in him, according to the grace of our God and the Lord Jesus Christ.

* **Question 1:** What do you think is meant by "work of faith" in these passages? Note other phrases that are used in the context.

Look again at 1 Thessalonians 1:2–3 and 2 Thessalonians 1:11–12.

Question 2: Is the work of faith something that we do or something that God does? Why is this question not simple? (Look carefully at 2 Thessalonians 1:11–12, noting the purpose of Paul's prayer.)

DAY 2—WHAT COUNTS WITH GOD

Some people think that James and Paul disagree on the doctrine of justification by faith. They do so on the basis of Paul's teaching in Romans 3–5 and James's teaching in James 2.

Read Romans 3:28 and Romans 4:1–8.

For we hold that one is justified by faith apart from works of the law.

¹What then shall we say was gained by Abraham, our forefather according to the flesh? ²For if Abraham was justified by works, he has something to boast about, but not before God. ³For what does the Scripture say? "Abraham believed God, and it was counted to him as righteousness." ⁴Now to the one who works, his wages are not counted as a gift but as his due. ⁵And to the one who does not work but believes in him who justifies the ungodly, his faith is counted as righteousness, ⁶just as David also speaks of the blessing of the one to whom God counts righteousness apart from works:

⁷"Blessed are those whose lawless deeds are forgiven,
    and whose sins are covered;
⁸blessed is the man against whom the Lord will not count his sin."

Now read James 2:14–26.

¹⁴What good is it, my brothers, if someone says he has faith but does not have works? Can that faith save him? ¹⁵If a brother or sister is poorly clothed and lacking in daily food, ¹⁶and one of you says to them, "Go in peace, be warmed and filled," without giving them the things needed for the body, what good is that? ¹⁷So also faith by itself, if it does not have works, is dead.

¹⁸But someone will say, "You have faith and I have works." Show me your faith apart from your works, and I will show you my faith by my works. ¹⁹You believe that God is one; you do well. Even the demons believe—and shudder! ²⁰Do you want to be shown, you foolish person, that faith apart from works is useless? ²¹Was not Abraham our father justified by works when he offered up his son Isaac on the altar? ²²You see that faith was active along with his works, and faith was completed by his works; ²³and the Scripture was fulfilled that says, "Abraham believed God, and it was counted to him as righteousness"—and he was called a friend of God. ²⁴You see that a person is justified by works and not by faith alone. ²⁵And in the same way was not also Rahab the

prostitute justified by works when she received the messengers and sent them out by another way? [26]For as the body apart from the spirit is dead, so also faith apart from works is dead.

* **Question 3:** Attempt to reconcile the teaching of Paul and James in these passages. What issues do you think that Paul is addressing? What issue do you think that James is addressing? Do you think that they disagree with each other? Why or why not?

Now read Galatians 5:5–6.

[5]For through the Spirit, by faith, we ourselves eagerly wait for the hope of righteousness. [6]For in Christ Jesus neither circumcision nor uncircumcision counts for anything, but only faith working through love.

Question 4: What type of faith counts before God? How does this faith relate to the hope of righteousness? How might this verse help to resolve the tension between James and Paul?

DAY 3—THE GRACE OF GOD

All Christians embrace the reality that the grace of God saves us. "For by grace you have been saved through faith" (Ephesians 2:8). But not all Christians are aware that grace is more than pardon; it is power.

Meditate on 1 Corinthians 15:10.

> But by the grace of God I am what I am, and his grace toward me
> was not in vain. On the contrary, I worked harder than any of
> them, though it was not I, but the grace of God that is with me.

> * **Question 5:** Identify the paradox of grace in this passage. How
> does this passage demonstrate that grace is power?

Paul begins and ends all thirteen of his letters in a similar way. While
there are some variations, there are certain elements that are always there.
Given this consistency, it is worth asking whether there is some larger
point being communicated by his greetings and his closing words. We
will use 1 Corinthians as a test case.

Read 1 Corinthians 1:3 and 16:23.

> Grace to you and peace from God our Father and the Lord Jesus
> Christ.

> The grace of the Lord Jesus be with you.

> **Question 6**: What elements both begin and end the letter? What
> differences do you notice? What do you think is the signifi-
> cance of these differences? (If need be, compare what you see
> in 1 Corinthians with Paul's other letters.)

Day 4—Grace as Power

Study 2 Corinthians 12:7–10.

> [7]So to keep me from becoming conceited because of the surpassing greatness of the revelations, a thorn was given me in the flesh, a messenger of Satan to harass me, to keep me from becoming conceited. [8]Three times I pleaded with the Lord about this, that it should leave me. [9]But he said to me, "My grace is sufficient for you, for my power is made perfect in weakness." Therefore I will boast all the more gladly of my weaknesses, so that the power of Christ may rest upon me. [10]For the sake of Christ, then, I am content with weaknesses, insults, hardships, persecutions, and calamities. For when I am weak, then I am strong.

Question 7: Why was Paul given a thorn in his flesh? Why did God not remove it? What are the weaknesses that Paul mentions in verse 10?

* **Question 8**: What is the relationship between grace and power in 2 Corinthians 12:7–10?

Day 5—A Comprehensive Promise

In the midst of discussion about generosity and giving, Paul makes one of the most sweeping promises in the Bible.

Read 2 Corinthians 9:8.

> And God is able to make all grace abound to you, so that having all sufficiency in all things at all times, you may abound in every good work.

> **Question 9:** Underline everything that makes this promise comprehensive. What areas of your life can you apply this promise to right now?

In future lessons, we will study the relationship between gratitude for past grace and faith in future grace. For now, we will look at one passage that highlights this relationship.

Reflect on 2 Timothy 4:17–18.

> [17]But the Lord stood by me and strengthened me, so that through me the message might be fully proclaimed and all the Gentiles might hear it. So I was rescued from the lion's mouth. [18]The Lord will rescue me from every evil deed and bring me safely into his heavenly kingdom. To him be the glory forever and ever. Amen.

> * **Question 10:** Underline references to past grace. Circle references to future grace. What do you think Paul means by "the lion's mouth"? What evil deeds do you think Paul believes God will rescue him from? Explain your answer.

FURTHER UP AND FURTHER IN

Read or listen to "I Act the Miracle," an online sermon at the Desiring God website.

> **Question 11:** In what three ways does the cross of Jesus Christ deal with sin?

> **Question 12:** According to John Piper, what is the link between the cross and our conquered sin? What is the power that establishes this link? Note the biblical support for this link and this power.

> **Question 13:** What new insights did Piper see in Philippians 2:12–13?

> **Question 14:** What does Piper mean by "I act the miracle"? Explain this phrase in your own words.

Question 15: In what area of your life can you apply the teaching of this sermon? Be specific and look for opportunities to act the miracle.

→ *While You Watch the DVD, Take Notes* ←

Faith is the _____.

Biblical support:

I _____ the miracle.

According to John Piper, why does Paul begin and end his letters in the way he does?

What does John Piper think is meant by the phrase "every good work" in 2 Corinthians 9:8?

What does Piper think Paul means by "the lion's mouth" and "every evil deed" in 2 Timothy 4:17–18?

→ *After You Watch the DVD, Discuss What You've Learned* ←

1. After completing this lesson, how would you connect the power of God to our faith in his promises? What remaining questions do you have?

2. What does John Piper mean by "I act the miracle"? Where else in the Bible might you find support for this notion?

3. Discuss any current or upcoming concerns, fears, weaknesses, hardships, etc. As you mention your various struggles, encourage each other with promises and with prayer.

—✦ *After You Discuss, Make Application* ✦—

1. What was the most meaningful part of this lesson for you? Was there a sentence, concept, or idea that really struck you? Why? Record your thoughts in the space below.

2. Memorize 2 Corinthians 9:8 this week and seek opportunities to apply it in your life or in the lives of those close to you.

WHAT IS FAITH?

A Companion Study to the Future Grace *DVD, Session 6*

LESSON OBJECTIVES

It is our prayer that after you have finished this lesson…
- You will be able to explain how the marriage metaphor is used in the New Testament.
- You will be able to make some comments on the meaning of Ephesians 5:22–33.
- You will grasp the beauty of marriage and understand its deepest purpose.

→* *Before You Watch the DVD, Study and Prepare* *←

DAY 1—UNION WITH CHRIST

The doctrine of union with Christ is perhaps the best way to summarize the New Testament's teaching on salvation. Union with Christ pervades the pages of the New Testament and undergirds every aspect of our salvation. In particular, union with Christ by faith is connected to both our justification and our sanctification. In this lesson we begin with an excerpt from the Bethlehem Baptist Church Elder Affirmation of Faith on justification and sanctification, Section 10, available at hopeingod.org:

10.1 We believe that justification and sanctification are both brought about by God through faith, but not in the same way. Justification is an act of God's imputing and reckoning; sanctification is an act of God's imparting and transforming. Thus the function of faith in regard to each is different. In regard to justification, faith is not the channel through which power or transformation flows to the soul of the believer, but rather faith is the occasion of God's forgiving, acquitting, and reckoning as righteous. But in regard to sanctification, faith is indeed the channel through which divine power and transformation flow to the soul; and the sanctifying work of God through faith does indeed touch the soul and change it into the likeness of Christ.

* **Question 1:** Summarize in your own words how justification by faith is different from sanctification by faith.

Now study Romans 8:9–11.

[9] You, however, are not in the flesh but in the Spirit, if in fact the Spirit of God dwells in you. Anyone who does not have the Spirit of Christ does not belong to him. [10] But if Christ is in you, although the body is dead because of sin, the Spirit is life because of righteousness. [11] If the Spirit of him who raised Jesus from the dead dwells in you, he who raised Christ Jesus from the dead will also give life to your mortal bodies through his Spirit who dwells in you.

Question 2: Underline every reference to someone dwelling or being "in" us. What effect does this indwelling have on us?

DAY 2—FAITH LOOKS BACK, OUT, AND FORWARD

Recall the discussion of the past, present, and future in Lesson 2. When put in terms of faith, faith can look back to the past, out in the present, and forward to the future.

Question 3: Give examples of faith looking back, faith looking out, and faith looking forward in your own life. Now try to connect your faith in past grace to the present and future (and vice versa).

Examine Romans 5:9–10.

[9]Since, therefore, we have now been justified by his blood, much more shall we be saved by him from the wrath of God. [10]For if while we were enemies we were reconciled to God by the death of his Son, much more, now that we are reconciled, shall we be saved by his life.

* **Question 4:** Underline examples of past grace in this passage. Circle examples of present grace. Put a box around examples of future grace. What is the argument of the passage?

DAY 3—SUSTAINED IN PRESENT DISTRESS

Faith in future grace is no mere academic exercise. Rather, it is what sustains us when we are faced with hardship, distress, and pain in the present. The Bible repeatedly emphasizes this future dimension of faith.

Read Romans 4:19–21.

[19]He did not weaken in faith when he considered his own body, which was as good as dead (since he was about a hundred years old), or when he considered the barrenness of Sarah's womb. [20]No unbelief made him waver concerning the promise of God, but he grew strong in his faith as he gave glory to God, [21]fully convinced that God was able to do what he had promised.

* **Question 5:** What hardships did Abraham and Sarah face in this passage? What prevented him from becoming weak in faith? What was the result of his faith?

Paul didn't just use others as examples of faith in future grace in the midst of trials; he practiced such faith himself.

Read 2 Corinthians 1:8–9.

> [8]For we do not want you to be unaware, brothers, of the affliction we experienced in Asia. For we were so utterly burdened beyond our strength that we despaired of life itself. [9]Indeed, we felt that we had received the sentence of death. But that was to make us rely not on ourselves but on God who raises the dead.

Question 6: How does Paul describe his afflictions in this passage? What words emphasize the intensity of his trials? What future grace sustained him through these trials?

Day 4—The Power of Faith to Transform

Stressing the future orientation of faith can help us to understand its power to transform us. In fact, it's often our failure to truly embrace future grace that leads us into all manner of sins in the present.

Look closely at 1 Corinthians 3:1–4.

> [1]But I, brothers, could not address you as spiritual people, but as people of the flesh, as infants in Christ. [2]I fed you with milk, not solid food, for you were not ready for it. And even now you are not yet ready, [3]for you are still of the flesh. For while there is jealousy and strife among you, are you not of the flesh and behaving only in a human way? [4]For when one says, "I follow Paul," and another, "I follow Apollos," are you not being merely human?

Question 7: Describe the sin of the Corinthians. What sins are mastering them and why?

Now look at 1 Corinthians 3:21–23, where Paul seeks to address their sin.

²¹So let no one boast in men. For all things are yours, ²²whether Paul or Apollos or Cephas or the world or life or death or the present or the future—all are yours, ²³and you are Christ's, and Christ is God's.

* **Question 8:** What sin does Paul identify in them? What truth does he set before them in order to overcome this temptation? Describe how you think this truth combats the sin that they are being mastered by?

Day 5—Faith: Assent, Trust, or Delight?

Earlier in this study we've explored some tensions between the biblical teaching on justification by faith and the necessity of good works. We noted that Christians sometimes disagree over the proper way to resolve this tension. A central component of that disagreement is the definition of faith.

* **Question 9:** Which of the following statements best reflects your view of faith? If none of them do, write your own.

    A. Faith is the assent of our minds to truth claims, such as the historical claim that Jesus rose from the dead.

    B. Faith is the assent of our minds to truth claims, as well as trust in the one making the claim.

    C. Faith includes both mental assent and trust, but also includes a sense of delight and joy in the truth being put forth.

    D. Faith includes mental assent, trust, delight, as well as the good works that we do.

One of the clearest explanations of faith in the gospels is given by Jesus in John 6.

Think carefully about John 6:35.

Jesus said to them, "I am the bread of life; whoever comes to me shall not hunger, and whoever believes in me shall never thirst.

Question 10: What is the parallel to believing in this verse? Formulate a definition of faith based on this verse.

FURTHER UP AND FURTHER IN

Read an online article, "Fact! Faith! Feeling!" at the Desiring God website.

Question 11: Summarize in your own words the meaning of the slogan "Fact! Faith! Feeling!" What is your initial reaction to it?

Question 12: What problem does John Piper see in this slogan? What addition does he want to make to receiving Christ as Savior and Lord? Do you agree with his emphasis?

Question 13: Have you ever been in a situation where leaders have been a flashpoint for pride and division? Record some reflections on what you think caused the division.

Read or listen to "I Planted, Apollos Watered, but God Gave the Growth," an online sermon at the Desiring God website.

Question 14: According to Piper, how does Paul address God and human leadership so as to promote humility and overcome pride and division? Which truth that Piper mentions would have been most relevant in your situation?

Read or listen to "The Faith-Grace-Certainty Connection," an online sermon at the Desiring God website.

Question 15: Summarize in your own words the faith-grace-certainty connection.

—• *While You Watch the DVD, Take Notes* •—

How should a husband and father lead his family when his tank is
    empty?

What two things happen in union with Christ?

Faith is _____ and _____ future-oriented.

Biblical support:

Summarize the story told by John Newton.

Faith is _____ with _____ to be
    _____.

Biblical support:

—⋆ *After You Watch the DVD, Discuss What You've Learned* ⋆—

1. Discuss the difference between God's work in justification and God's work in sanctification, noting how the role of faith differs in each. If necessary, refer to Question 1 in this lesson.

2. Discuss the past, present, and future dimensions to faith, giving examples of each. Do you agree that faith is primarily future-oriented? Why or why not?

3. What is the affectional element in faith? Why is this element so crucial for us to remember and emphasize?

—⋆ *After You Discuss, Make Application* ⋆—

1. What was the most meaningful part of this lesson for you? Was there a sentence, concept, or idea that really struck you? Why? Record your thoughts in the space below.

2. Spend some time praying about applying the teaching on living
    by faith in future grace in your own home. If you are the head
    of your household, pray about ways to bring this into your
    family. If you are not, pray about ways to suggest to your hus-
    band or father how to increase the family's faith.

LESSON 7

THE CRUCIAL FUNCTION OF BYGONE GRACE

A Companion Study to the Future Grace *DVD, Session 7*

LESSON OBJECTIVES

It is our prayer that after you have finished this lesson…
- You will embrace the crucial role of bygone grace in promoting faith in future grace.
- You will rest in the solid logic of heaven.
- You will have a deeper understanding of the way in which the Holy Spirit produces love.

→ *Before You Watch the DVD, Study and Prepare* ←

DAY 1—THE PRESENT POWER OF PAST GRACE

The bulk of this study guide thus far has focused on the way that faith in *future* grace produces holiness in our lives. It's possible to get the impression from this emphasis that past grace is largely irrelevant to living a life of love. However, nothing could be further from the truth. The next two lessons explore the crucial role that past grace plays in transforming us into Christlike people.

> * **Question 1:** Based on what you've learned thus far, how would you describe the role of past grace in the Christian life? How does it promote holiness?

Read Galatians 2:20 and Romans 5:8.

> I have been crucified with Christ. It is no longer I who live, but Christ who lives in me. And the life I now live in the flesh I live by faith in the Son of God, who loved me and gave himself for me.

> But God shows his love for us in that while we were still sinners, Christ died for us.

> **Question 2:** Underline every present tense verb in these passages. Circle every example of past grace. What do you notice about the relationship between past grace and our present experience?

DAY 2—THE GLORIOUS ARGUMENT OF ROMANS 8:32

John Piper has said that Romans 8:32 may be his favorite verse in the entire Bible. The reason that this verse is so precious to him is because of the argument that Paul makes in it.

Read Romans 8:31–34.

> [31]What then shall we say to these things? If God is for us, who can be against us? [32]He who did not spare his own Son but gave him up for us all, how will he not also with him graciously give us all things? [33]Who shall bring any charge against God's elect? It is God who justifies. [34]Who is to condemn? Christ Jesus is the one who died—more than that, who was raised—who is at the right hand of God, who indeed is interceding for us.

Question 3: These verses contain a number of different rhetorical questions that have an implied and obvious answer. Rewrite each rhetorical question in the form of a statement (e.g., "Because God is for us, no one can be against us").

Look carefully at Romans 8:32 and your restatement of it.

* **Question 4:** Make up a sentence that would use the same logical structure as Romans 8:32. The statement can be about anything; the key is to understand the logic of the passage.

DAY 3—A SYMPATHETIC HIGH PRIEST

Meditate on Hebrews 4:14–16.

> [14]Since then we have a great high priest who has passed through the heavens, Jesus, the Son of God, let us hold fast our confession.

¹⁵For we do not have a high priest who is unable to sympathize with our weaknesses, but one who in every respect has been tempted as we are, yet without sin. ¹⁶Let us then with confidence draw near to the throne of grace, that we may receive mercy and find grace to help in time of need.

* **Question 5:** Underline the two main exhortations in this passage. Identify the ground of these exhortations. In other words, what truth (or truths) gives rise to these exhortations?

Paul teaches that Christ came into the world to confirm the promises of God (Romans 15:8). Indeed, all the promises of God are "Yes" in him (2 Corinthians 1:20). But this raises a question, are the promises of God unconditional? Do we automatically receive them when we become believers? Or are some of the promises conditional?

Study James 4:6–8 and 1 Peter 5:6.

⁶But he gives more grace. Therefore it says, "God opposes the proud, but gives grace to the humble." ⁷Submit yourselves therefore to God. Resist the devil, and he will flee from you. ⁸Draw near to God, and he will draw near to you. Cleanse your hands, you sinners, and purify your hearts, you double-minded.

Humble yourselves, therefore, under the mighty hand of God so that at the proper time he may exalt you.

Question 6: Identify any promises in these verses. What conditions must be met before the promises are realized?

DAY 4—THE ROLE OF THE HOLY SPIRIT

We have seen that it is faith that produces love (Galatians 5:6; 1 Timothy 1:5). However, the Bible also teaches that love is the fruit of the Holy Spirit (Galatians 5:22). So how does the Holy Spirit work with faith to produce love?

Examine Galatians 3:1–5.

> ¹O foolish Galatians! Who has bewitched you? It was before your eyes that Jesus Christ was publicly portrayed as crucified. ²Let me ask you only this: Did you receive the Spirit by works of the law or by hearing with faith? ³Are you so foolish? Having begun by the Spirit, are you now being perfected by the flesh? ⁴Did you suffer so many things in vain—if indeed it was in vain? ⁵Does he who supplies the Spirit to you and works miracles among you do so by works of the law, or by hearing with faith?

* **Question 7:** According to this passage, how does the Holy Spirit come to us? Underline the relevant phrase. What do you think this phrase means?

The key phrase in Galatians 3:1–5 is "hearing with faith."

Question 8: Why do you think that Paul says that we receive the
Spirit by *hearing* with faith, rather than simply saying that
we receive the Spirit by faith (as he does in Galatians 3:14)?
What does the word *hearing* emphasize? What do you think
is heard?

Now why does he say "by *hearing* with faith" instead of
just "by faith"? The Spirit comes and works mightily in
our lives, killing sin, not just "by faith" but by "*hearing*
with faith." Why does he say it that way? The answer is
that the sword of the Spirit is the word of God, and it's
the word that you hear and believe. When the word of
God—the Sword of the Spirit—is heard and believed, the
Spirit is moving with vigorous, sin-killing action.

In other words, the connection between the Holy Spirit and you is
the word of God and faith. They are like socket and plug. When the plug
of your faith goes in the socket of God's Word, the Spirit is flowing. And
when he flows, he kills sin.[8]

Day 5—The Mission
of the Holy Spirit

We've seen that the Holy Spirit comes to us by hearing with faith. We also
know that faith comes by hearing and hearing by the word of Christ
(Romans 10:17). Today we will explore why the Spirit links his work to
faith and the word in this way.

Look at John 15:26 and 16:13–14.

But when the Helper comes, whom I will send to you from the Father, the Spirit of truth, who proceeds from the Father, he will bear witness about me.

[13] When the Spirit of truth comes, he will guide you into all the truth, for he will not speak on his own authority, but whatever he hears he will speak, and he will declare to you the things that are to come. [14] He will glorify me, for he will take what is mine and declare it to you.

* **Question 9**: What is the mission of the Holy Spirit in these passages?

Question 10: In light of the Holy Spirit's mission, why do you think he links his work so closely to faith and the word of Christ?

FURTHER UP AND FURTHER IN

Read or listen to "The Solid Logic of Heaven Holds," an online sermon at the Desiring God website.

Question 11: Read through the various examples of the logic of heaven in Romans. Be sure that you understand the logic in each passage.

Question 12: What is a *fortiori* argument?

Question 13: What is the greatest obstacle to our salvation? How was this obstacle overcome?

Read "How Does the Spirit Produce Love?," an online article at the Desiring God website.

Question 14: According to John Piper, how does the Spirit produce love in us?

Question 15: According to Piper, why does the Spirit do it this way?

→❖ *While You Watch the DVD, Take Notes* ❖←

The importance of the present tense in Galatians 2:20 and
Romans 5:8:

What is "the solid logic of heaven"?

What is the role of personality in our expression of emotions and
affections?

Why is it important to preach against both libertines and legalists?

Why does the Spirit unite himself to faith to bring about love?

Because the Holy Spirit's _____ is to
_____, and so makes _____ in
_____-_____ the means by which
he works.

---⟶ *After You Watch the DVD, Discuss What You've Learned* ⟵---

1. Discuss "the solid logic of heaven." What is meant by a *fortiori* argument?

2. Have you ever used logic to reason with your soul in relation to some struggle or temptation? How can you improve in the use of such biblical logic?

3. Why is it so important that the Holy Spirit unites himself to promises in order to kill sin and produce love?

---⟶ *After You Discuss, Make Application* ⟵---

1. What was the most meaningful part of this lesson for you? Was there a sentence, concept, or idea that really struck you? Why? Record your thoughts in the space below.

2. This week explain "the solid logic of heaven" to someone that you know.

THE ROLE OF GRATITUDE IN PRODUCING OBEDIENCE

A Companion Study to the Future Grace *DVD, Session 8*

LESSON OBJECTIVES

It is our prayer that after you have finished this lesson...
- You will recognize the debtor's ethic when you meet it in your own soul or in others.
- You will embrace the proper role of gratitude in producing love and holiness.
- You will abound in thanksgiving and gratitude and thus increase your faith in future grace.

⟶ *Before You Watch the DVD, Study and Prepare* ✶⟵

DAY 1—THE JOY SET BEFORE HIM

The book of Hebrews describes Jesus as the founder of our salvation (2:10) and our faith (12:2). He is our forerunner (6:20), who has gone before us into the holy place as our high priest. To become such a high priest, he had to endure incredible suffering, pain, and death. Which raises the question: How did Jesus endure the cross?

Read Hebrews 12:1–2.

> [1]Therefore, since we are surrounded by so great a cloud of witnesses, let us also lay aside every weight, and sin which clings so closely, and let us run with endurance the race that is set before us, [2]looking to Jesus, the founder and perfecter of our faith, who for the joy that was set before him endured the cross, despising the shame, and is seated at the right hand of the throne of God.

Question 1: What exhortations to us are given in this passage? How did Jesus endure the pain and shame of the cross? Underline the key phrase.

* **Question 2:** In your opinion, is Jesus an example of living by faith in future grace in Hebrews 12:1–2? Explain your answer.

DAY 2—MOTIVATED BY GRATITUDE?

We've seen that bygone grace is the foundation of future grace in that the grace of God given in the life, death, and resurrection of Jesus purchased for us all of the blessings that we enjoy, both now and forever. We now turn to the question of gratitude: should Christians be motivated to obey God out of gratitude?

Question 3: Should Christians be motivated to obey God out of gratitude? Note any biblical passages that you think would have bearing on this question.

It's not uncommon for preachers to seek to motivate Christians to obedience based on gratitude. For example, a common exhortation might be, "God has done so much for you; now what will you do for him?" Or "He gave his life for you. Will you give your life for him?" Or "God has purchased you at the great cost of his Son. It is now your great privilege to spend the rest of your life paying him back through your heartfelt obedience."

* **Question 4:** Have you ever heard exhortations like those above? Record other similar ideas in the space below. What is your reaction to them? Do you find them helpful? biblical? motivating?

DAY 3—HOW CAN WE PAY GOD BACK?

The notion of rendering God obedience because he has done so much for you can be construed to mean that we are attempting to pay God back for all of his kindness to us. But what would such an effort look like?

Think carefully about Psalm 116:12–14.

> [12]What shall I render to the LORD
> for all his benefits to me?
> [13]I will lift up the cup of salvation
> and call on the name of the LORD,
> [14]I will pay my vows to the LORD
> in the presence of all his people.

* **Question 5:** According to this passage, how can we pay God
  back for all of his benefits to us? Explain what this payback
  means in your own words.

John Piper often says, "You can't run your car on gratitude for yesterday's gas."

Question 6: What do you think this phrase means? Attempt to
explain it in your own words.

DAY 4—WHAT MAKES GOD UNIQUE

The God of the Bible is utterly unique. The Scriptures proclaim this over
and over. "There is none like you, O LORD" (Jeremiah 10:6). "There is
none like you among the gods, O Lord" (Psalm 86:8). But what makes
God unique?

Study Romans 11:33–36.

³³Oh, the depth of the riches and wisdom and knowledge of God!
How unsearchable are his judgments and how inscrutable his ways!
   ³⁴"For who has known the mind of the Lord,
   or who has been his counselor?"
   ³⁵"Or who has given a gift to him
   that he might be repaid?"
³⁶For from him and through him and to him are all things. To
him be glory forever. Amen.

Question 7: What is the implied answer to Paul's questions?
   Rephrase verses 34–35 as statements. How does verse 36
   ground these statements?

Now read Isaiah 64:4 and 2 Chronicles 16:9.

From of old no one has heard or perceived by the ear, no eye has
seen a God besides you, who acts for those who wait for him.

For the eyes of the LORD run to and fro throughout the whole
earth, to give strong support to those whose heart is blameless
toward him.

Question 8: What makes God unique from other gods? What
   does the imagery of these passages suggest about God's desire
   to help his people?

This sets the God of the Bible off from all other gods.
Isaiah the prophet said,

From of old no one has heard or perceived by the
ear, no eye has seen a God besides you, who works for
those who wait for him. (Isaiah 64:4)

No one ever dreamed that God was like this. He had
to reveal it to us in the Bible. That the burden of God's
heart is to work for people, not to have them work for
him. Another place says,

The eyes of the LORD run to and fro throughout the
whole earth, to show his might in behalf of those whose
heart is whole toward him. (2 Chronicles 16:9)

In other words the Christian gospel is not a "Help
Wanted" sign. God is not looking for labor. He is looking
for people who magnify his power and wisdom and
love by admitting their needs and letting him labor for
them.[9]

DAY 5—A CONVERSATION BETWEEN GRATITUDE AND FAITH

The Scriptures are clear that gratitude is a crucial part of the Christian
life. "Give thanks to the LORD, for he is good, for his steadfast love endures forever" (Psalm 136:1). "All your works shall give thanks to you, O
LORD, and all your saints shall bless you!" (Psalm 145:10). "Give thanks
in all circumstances; for this is the will of God in Christ Jesus for you"
(1 Thessalonians 5:18). "Giving thanks always and for everything to
God the Father in the name of our Lord Jesus Christ" (Ephesians 5:20).
But how does gratitude relate to our faith, especially if our faith is funda-
mentally future-oriented?

Question 9: Write a hypothetical conversation in which Gratitude has a conversation with Faith in Future Grace. What would Gratitude say to Faith? What would Faith say to Gratitude?

* **Question 10:** Spend a few moments and make a list of twenty things that you are grateful for. They can be big things or little things. Be as specific and concrete as you can. For example, don't just say that you're thankful for your family; identify a specific characteristic that you are grateful for, such as "I'm grateful for my son's laughter."

Further Up and Further In

Read or listen to "Sustained by All His Grace," an online sermon at the Desiring God website.

Question 11: The first part of this sermon reiterates many of the themes that you've studied in previous lessons. Identify any new elements that helped to clarify key concepts for you.

Question 12: What two lessons does John Piper draw from his reflections on grace?

Read or listen to "For Freedom Christ Has Set Us Free," an online sermon at the Desiring God website.

Question 13: What is the "Gratitude Ethic"? According to John Piper, why is the gratitude ethic wrong?

Question 14: What two phrases does John Piper give for the acronym G.R.A.C.E.?

Read or listen to "Guard Yourself with Gratitude," an online sermon at the Desiring God website.

Question 15: How does gratitude guard the soul? What illustrations does John Piper give from Colossians?

—＊ *While You Watch the DVD, Take Notes* ＊—

Define the debtor's ethic:

What is the proper way to pay God back?

Reasons that the debtor's ethic is dangerous:

Reason 1:

Reason 2:

Reason 3:

How gratitude helps us obey Christ:

1.

2.

—❖ *After You Watch the DVD, Discuss What You've Learned* ❖—

1. Discuss the debtor's ethic. Have you ever used the debtor's ethic in your own life? Have you heard it preached from the pulpit? Do you agree that it is dangerous to think this way?

2. Discuss the proper role of gratitude in promoting obedience. Can you give any examples from your own life of the interwovenness of gratitude for past grace and faith in future grace?

3. Share your gratitude list from Question 10.

→❀ *After You Discuss, Make Application* ❀←

1. What was the most meaningful part of this lesson for you? Was there a sentence, concept, or idea that really struck you? Why? Record your thoughts in the space below.

2. Using your gratitude list from Question 10, initiate a conversation between Gratitude and Faith in Future Grace. Apply what you learned about gratitude to the list of present and future concerns that you made in Lesson 2.

HOW FAITH IN FUTURE GRACE PRODUCES RADICAL LOVE

A Companion Study to the Future Grace *DVD, Session 9*

LESSON OBJECTIVES

It is our prayer that after you have finished this lesson...

- You will recognize the biblical reasoning that can produce hard acts of love.
- You will grasp the proper relationship between reward-seeking and love.
- You will be able to encourage people who are struggling to love others.

—* *Before You Watch the DVD, Study and Prepare* *—

DAY 1—THE SERMON ON THE MOUNT

The ethical teaching of Jesus centers on the command to love. First, we are to love God with all that we are (Matthew 22:37–38). But Christian love also includes both the love of neighbors (Matthew 22:39) and love of enemies (Matthew 5:43–44).

Read Matthew 5:43–45.

[43]You have heard that it was said, "You shall love your neighbor and hate your enemy." [44]But I say to you, Love your enemies and pray for those who persecute you, [45]so that you may be sons of your Father who is in heaven. For he makes his sun rise on the evil and on the good, and sends rain on the just and on the unjust.

Question 1: In this passage, what does it mean to "love your enemies"? What parallel does Jesus highlight? Why should we love our enemies in this way?

So one of the main ways that we can love our enemies is through prayer for them.

Now look at Matthew 5:11–12.

[11]Blessed are you when others revile you and persecute you and utter all kinds of evil against you falsely on my account. [12]Rejoice and be glad, for your reward is great in heaven, for so they persecuted the prophets who were before you.

* **Question 2:** Which do you think is more difficult: to pray for those who persecute you, or to rejoice in your persecutions? Explain your answer.

DAY 2—THE GOLDEN RULE

The Golden Rule is perhaps one of the most widely known teachings of Jesus. But this command does not exist in a vacuum. Jesus gives this command in the midst of a larger argument. Let's look at the Golden Rule (Matthew 7:7–12) in context.

> [7]Ask, and it will be given to you; seek, and you will find; knock, and it will be opened to you. [8]For everyone who asks receives, and the one who seeks finds, and to the one who knocks it will be opened. [9]Or which one of you, if his son asks him for bread, will give him a stone? [10] Or if he asks for a fish, will give him a serpent? [11]If you then, who are evil, know how to give good gifts to your children, how much more will your Father who is in heaven give good things to those who ask him!
>
> [12]So whatever you wish that others would do to you, do also to them, for this is the Law and the Prophets.

Question 3: Underline the Golden Rule. What is the whole passage about? Summarize Jesus' argument in verses 9–11. What is his reasoning here?

* **Question 4:** The word *so* in verse 12 could also be translated "therefore." In this light, how does the command in verse 12 relate to the previous discussion of parental gifts? What is Jesus' logic?

DAY 3—SHOULD WE BE MOTIVATED BY REWARD?

One of the central claims of this study is that it is good and right for us to be motivated to love people by future reward. But some people object to this motivation.

> Immanuel Kant, the German philosopher who died in 1804, was the most powerful exponent of the notion that the moral value of an act decreases as we aim to derive any benefit from it. Acts are good if the doer is "disinterested." We should do the good because it is good. Any motivation to seek joy or reward corrupts the act.[10]

Even many Christians agree with Kant that loving someone in order to receive a reward from God reduces the moral worth of the act of love. Such "love," they say, is not real love. Real love does good to others for its own sake, and not for the sake of some future reward. Rewards may come as a by-product, but we should not aim for them.

> * **Question 5:** What do you think about the Kantian objection to reward-seeking? Does seeking reward as a motivation to love ruin the value of such love?

Look carefully at Luke 14:12–14.

> [12]He said also to the man who had invited him, "When you give a dinner or a banquet, do not invite your friends or your brothers or your relatives or rich neighbors, lest they also invite you in return and you be repaid. [13]But when you give a feast, invite the

poor, the crippled, the lame, the blind, [14]and you will be blessed, because they cannot repay you. For you will be repaid at the resurrection of the just."

Question 6: What bearing does this passage have on the previous discussion of our motivation to love? How does Jesus motivate us to love others?

DAY 4—THE EXAMPLE OF MOSES AND JESUS

In a previous lesson we looked at Jesus' example in Hebrews 12. But the book of Hebrews contains other examples of love in hard places. Consider first the example of Moses.

Read Hebrews 11:24–26.

[24]By faith Moses, when he was grown up, refused to be called the son of Pharaoh's daughter, [25]choosing rather to be mistreated with the people of God than to enjoy the fleeting pleasures of sin. [26]He considered the reproach of Christ greater wealth than the treasures of Egypt, for he was looking to the reward.

* **Question 7:** What choice did Moses face when he was grown up? Why did he make the hard choice to suffer with God's people?

Now look at Hebrews 13:12–14.

¹²So Jesus also suffered outside the gate in order to sanctify the people through his own blood. ¹³Therefore let us go to him outside the camp and bear the reproach he endured. ¹⁴For here we have no lasting city, but we seek the city that is to come.

Question 8: What do you think it means to "go to him outside the camp"? How does the author of Hebrews motivate us to do this? Underline the relevant phrase.

DAY 5—HELPING OTHERS IN PAIN

We hope that one of the results of this study is that you will be better equipped to help others who are struggling to love in difficult circumstances or who are undergoing serious hardship or suffering. Today's questions invite you to reflect on how you would encourage people in such difficult situations.

Look again at Matthew 7:9–11.

⁹Or which one of you, if his son asks him for bread, will give him a stone? ¹⁰Or if he asks for a fish, will give him a serpent? ¹¹If you then, who are evil, know how to give good gifts to your children, how much more will your Father who is in heaven give good things to those who ask him!

* **Question 9:** How would you help someone who feels as though God really is giving them a stone? Perhaps they have asked him for a particular blessing, or have asked for God to relieve some suffering, and up to this point, he has not. What would you say to encourage them?

Question 10: How would you encourage a parent who uses the debtor's ethic on his or her children? In other words, this parent attempts to motivate the children to obey by saying, "I provide food on the table and a roof over your heads, in addition to a thousand other gifts. The least you could do was to do what I say." What would you say to this parent?

FURTHER UP AND FURTHER IN

Read "Christian Hedonism: Forgive the Label, but Don't Miss the Truth," an online article at the Desiring God website.

Question 11: According to Piper, why is disinterested love impossible?

Question 12: Make a chart contrasting Kantian morality with
biblical morality.

**Read or listen to "Liberated for Love by Looking to the Reward," an
online sermon at the Desiring God website.**

Question 13: Identify the four crisis points in Moses's life. How
was Moses (or his parents) able to endure each of these crises?

**Read or listen to "Who Should We Invite to Thanksgiving Din-
ner?" an online sermon at the Desiring God website.**

Question 14: What is the Law of Reciprocity? How does Jesus
challenge this "law"?

Question 15: According to Piper, how do we as Christians
sometimes mute the teaching of this passage? Have you ever
done this?

→• *While You Watch the DVD, Take Notes* •←

According to John Piper, is it harder to pray for your persecutors or
to rejoice in persecutions?

What is John Piper's definition of love?

Summarize how the argument of Matthew 7 (Golden Rule)
works:

How does John Piper respond to the objection that Jesus' teaching
in Luke 14 is selfish?

What advice does John Piper give to the debtor's ethic–driven
parent?

→* *After You Watch the DVD, Discuss What You've Learned* *←

1. Discuss the common theme of this lesson, namely, how the Bible motivates us to love in hard circumstances.

2. Discuss the objection to being motivated to love by the promise of reward. What lingering questions do you have about reward-seeking and love?

3. Discuss any current situations where you can encourage someone who is struggling to love others. In light of what you've learned, what could you say to them?

→* *After You Discuss, Make Application* *←

1. What was the most meaningful part of this lesson for you? Was there a sentence, concept, or idea that really struck you? Why? Record your thoughts in the space below.

2. Seek to apply Luke 14:12–14 in the next few weeks by inviting someone to dinner that you would not normally invite. Pray with your family or roommates about this invitation and make the effort to apply Jesus' words, knowing that you will be repaid at the resurrection.

FUTURE GRACE VERSUS ANXIETY AND COVETOUSNESS

A Companion Study to the Future Grace *DVD, Session 10*

LESSON OBJECTIVES

It is our prayer that after you have finished this lesson...

- You will be equipped to combat the sins of anxiety and covetousness in your own life.
- You will be encouraged by the all-sufficient provision of God for your every need.
- You will have a deeper understanding of the role of physical factors such as sleep, food, and medication in fighting sin.

—* *Before You Watch the DVD, Study and Prepare* *—

DAY 1—ASSESSING ANXIETY

In the next two lessons, we will apply what we have learned about faith in future grace to a number of particular sins. Today we begin with anxiety.

* **Question 1:** Define anxiety. What produces anxiety in your own
life? Make a list.

Question 2: What strategies do you currently employ in your fight
with anxiety? Which biblical passages do you turn to?

Day 2—All These Things Will Be Added

Jesus devotes an entire section of the Sermon on the Mount to the fight
with anxiety. In it, he provides a number of encouragements to us to be
free from anxiety.

Study Matthew 6:25–33.

> [25]Therefore I tell you, do not be anxious about your life, what you
> will eat or what you will drink, nor about your body, what you
> will put on. Is not life more than food, and the body more than
> clothing? [26]Look at the birds of the air: they neither sow nor reap
> nor gather into barns, and yet your heavenly Father feeds them.
> Are you not of more value than they? [27]And which of you by
> being anxious can add a single hour to his span of life? [28]And why
> are you anxious about clothing? Consider the lilies of the field,
> how they grow: they neither toil nor spin, [29]yet I tell you, even
> Solomon in all his glory was not arrayed like one of these. [30]But if
> God so clothes the grass of the field, which today is alive and

tomorrow is thrown into the oven, will he not much more clothe you, O you of little faith? [31]Therefore do not be anxious, saying, "What shall we eat?" or "What shall we drink?" or "What shall we wear?" [32]For the Gentiles seek after all these things, and your heavenly Father knows that you need them all. [33]But seek first the kingdom of God and his righteousness, and all these things will be added to you.

* **Question 3:** What are the main areas of anxiety that Jesus addresses in this passage? List the reasons that Jesus gives for us to be free from anxiety. Choose one of his arguments and unpack it in detail.

Look again at Matthew 6:32–33.

[32]For the Gentiles seek after all these things, and your heavenly Father knows that you need them all. [33]But seek first the kingdom of God and his righteousness, and all these things will be added to you.

Question 4: What do you think Jesus means by "all these things"? Does this passage teach that Christians who seek the kingdom will never lack food, clothing, and shelter? If not, what does it mean?

DAY 3—NEW MERCIES

The section from the Sermon on the Mount that we explored in the previous day's assignment ends with one more exhortation against anxiety.

Reflect on Matthew 6:34.

> Therefore do not be anxious about tomorrow, for tomorrow will be anxious for itself. Sufficient for the day is its own trouble.

Now look at Lamentations 3:21–24.

> [21]But this I call to mind,
>   and therefore I have hope:
> [22]The steadfast love of the LORD never ceases;
>   his mercies never come to an end;
> [23]they are new every morning;
>   great is your faithfulness.
> [24]"The LORD is my portion," says my soul,
>   "therefore I will hope in him."

> **Question 5**: According to Matthew 6:34, why should we not be anxious about tomorrow? What connection can you make to Lamentations 3?

Why are they new every morning? Why does God do it that way? It's not because yesterday's mercies were bad or weak. It's because they were yesterday's. Yesterday's mercies were for yesterday's burdens. Today's mercies are for today's burdens. They are new every morning. They are like the manna in the wilderness: you can't keep it overnight. Enough comes for each day. You live on God day by day, or you don't live on God.... So we must not compound today's load with fretting over tomorrow's. We must not doubt God and say, "I have no more strength; so tomorrow will be impossible to live." That's not true. You will not be asked to live tomorrow on today's strength. What you need today is not tomorrow's strength, but today's faith that tomorrow's mercies will be new and will be enough.[11]

In the contemporary world, it's difficult to discuss anxiety without discussing medication. Panic attacks, depression, and severe anxiety can cripple even the most faithful of Christians.

* **Question 6:** In your mind, how should Christians think about the use of medications to treat panic attacks, severe anxiety, and depression? Should Christians use a physical remedy (medication) to treat a spiritual problem?

DAY 4—DO NOT COVET

We turn now to a consideration of covetousness and greed.

* **Question 7:** Define covetousness. Describe your own struggle with covetousness and greed. What do you covet? What strategies do you use to combat covetousness in your own life?

Look carefully at Hebrews 13:5–6.

⁵Keep your life free from love of money, and be content with what you have, for he has said, "I will never leave you nor forsake you." ⁶So we can confidently say,

"The Lord is my helper;
I will not fear;
what can man do to me?"

Question 8: The argument of this passage is not obvious. How does the promise of the second half of verse 5 and all of verse 6 relate to the command? Attempt to explain how the logic of this passage works.

DAY 5—I CAN DO ALL THINGS THROUGH HIM WHO STRENGTHENS ME

One of the most oft-quoted verses in the Bible is found in Philippians 4:13. "I can do all things through him who strengthens me." This passage can be found on bumper stickers and posters, in the mouths of athletes and celebrities, and in a myriad of other places. But what does this passage actually mean in context?

Study Philippians 4:11–13.

¹¹Not that I am speaking of being in need, for I have learned in whatever situation I am to be content. ¹²I know how to be brought low, and I know how to abound. In any and every circumstance, I have learned the secret of facing plenty and

hunger, abundance and need. [13]I can do all things through him who strengthens me.

Question 9: What is this passage about? What are the "all things" that Paul is discussing in this passage?

While most of this study has focused on the promises of God that enable us to fight sin, it is also worth utilizing the warnings of Scripture. Warnings are the flip side of promises, motivating us by showing us what will happen if we fail to trust in future grace.

Study 1 Timothy 6:6–10.

[6]But godliness with contentment is great gain, [7]for we brought nothing into the world, and we cannot take anything out of the world. [8]But if we have food and clothing, with these we will be content. [9]But those who desire to be rich fall into temptation, into a snare, into many senseless and harmful desires that plunge people into ruin and destruction. [10]For the love of money is a root of all kinds of evils. It is through this craving that some have wandered away from the faith and pierced themselves with many pangs.

* **Question 10:** In this passage, what is the great danger of the desire to be rich? What do you think Paul means by "many pangs"? Be specific.

Further Up and Further In

Read or listen to "Do Not Be Anxious About Your Life," an online sermon at the Desiring God website.

> **Question 11:** Which of the struggles with anxiety mentioned by John Piper resonate with you?

> **Question 12:** Which of the eight reasons had you noticed when you did your own study of Matthew 6 in Day 2? Which ones were new? Which one was the most encouraging or challenging to you?

Read the following passages.

> Therefore, my beloved brothers, be steadfast, immovable, always abounding in the work of the Lord, knowing that in the Lord your labor is not in vain. (1 Corinthians 15:58)

> I will instruct you and teach you in the way you should go;
> I will counsel you with my eye upon you. (Psalm 32:8)

> [3]Listen to me, O house of Jacob,
> all the remnant of the house of Israel,
> who have been borne by me from before your birth,
> carried from the womb;

[4]even to your old age I am he,
    and to gray hairs I will carry you.
I have made, and I will bear;
    I will carry and will save. (Isaiah 46:3–4)

[7]For none of us lives to himself, and none of us dies to himself. [8]If we live, we live to the Lord, and if we die, we die to the Lord. So then, whether we live or whether we die, we are the Lord's. [9]For to this end Christ died and lived again, that he might be Lord both of the dead and of the living. (Romans 14:7–9)

Question 13: Identify a specific anxiety or situation that each passage could be useful for. Choose one and reflect on how this passage can encourage us to not be anxious about that specific situation or issue.

Read or listen to "Discerning Idolatry in Desire," an online sermon at the Desiring God website.

Question 14: Reflect on the first six tests of idolatry. Identify the ones that are most relevant to your life. Be specific.

Question 15: Reflect on the last six tests of idolatry. Identify the ones that are most relevant to your life. Be specific.

→ *While You Watch the DVD, Take Notes* ←

Anxiety: The loss of _____ _____ in God
    owing to feelings of _____ or _____
    that something _____ is going to happen.

According to John Piper, what are the "all these things" in Matthew
    6:33?

What connection does John Piper draw between Matthew 6:34
    and Lamentations 3:22–23?

Covetousness: _____ something not for _____
    _____ or in such a way that we lose our
    _____ in God as our _____
    _____.

What is the argument of Hebrews 13:5–6?

What bodily factors can affect our ability to combat anxiety?

→• *After You Watch the DVD, Discuss What You've Learned* •←

1. Discuss John Piper's understanding of the "all things" of Matthew 6:33 and Philippians 4:13. Were you persuaded by his explanation? What remaining questions do you have?

2. Discuss your struggle with anxiety. What practical strategies have you learned from this lesson to help you fight this sin? Include any discussion of the bodily factors that affect our ability to kill anxiety.

3. Discuss your struggle with covetousness. What practical strategies have you learned from this lesson to help you fight this sin?

→* *After You Discuss, Make Application* *←

1. What was the most meaningful part of this lesson for you? Was there a sentence, concept, or idea that really struck you? Why? Record your thoughts in the space below.

2. Memorize Lamentations 3:22–23 (or another passage related to anxiety) and Philippians 4:11–13 (or another passage related to covetousness). Make use of them as you confront the temptation to be anxious or greedy in the future.

FUTURE GRACE VERSUS LUST, BITTERNESS, AND IMPATIENCE

A Companion Study to the Future Grace *DVD, Session 11*

LESSON OBJECTIVES

It is our prayer that after you have finished this lesson…
- You will embrace the truth that you must be killing sin or sin will be killing you.
- You will be equipped to combat the sins of lust, bitterness, and impatience in your own life.
- You will receive future grace that will enable you to apply what you've learned to other sins besides those covered in this study.

--* ***Before You Watch the DVD, Study and Prepare*** *--

DAY 1—THE BATTLE AGAINST SEXUAL IMMORALITY

In this lesson, we will tackle three more sins by seeking to live by faith in future grace. The first sin is sexual lust.

Question 1: Define sexual lust in broad terms. In what ways do you struggle with sexual temptation? What strategies are you currently using in your fight against this sin?

There is a common thread in many of the biblical passages that describe the origins of sexual immorality.

Look closely at Ephesians 4:17–22 and 1 Thessalonians 4:3–5.

[17]Now this I say and testify in the Lord, that you must no longer walk as the Gentiles do, in the futility of their minds. [18]They are darkened in their understanding, alienated from the life of God because of the ignorance that is in them, due to their hardness of heart. [19]They have become callous and have given themselves up to sensuality, greedy to practice every kind of impurity. [20]But that is not the way you learned Christ!—[21]assuming that you have heard about him and were taught in him, as the truth is in Jesus, [22]to put off your old self, which belongs to your former manner of life and is corrupt through deceitful desires.

[3]For this is the will of God, your sanctification: that you abstain from sexual immorality; [4]that each one of you know how to control his own body in holiness and honor, [5]not in the passion of lust like the Gentiles who do not know God.

* **Question 2:** Underline every phrase in this passage that indicates where sexual immorality and lustful passions come from. What common themes emerge?

DAY 2—ESCAPE FROM CORRUPTION

Sexual sin provides one of the clearest examples of the way that faith in future grace overcomes temptation.

Read 2 Peter 1:3–4.

> ³His divine power has granted to us all things that pertain to life and godliness, through the knowledge of him who called us to his own glory and excellence, ⁴by which he has granted to us his precious and very great promises, so that through them you may become partakers of the divine nature, having escaped from the corruption that is in the world because of sinful desire.

> * **Question 3:** Trace the thought of this passage. How do we escape from the corruption in the world? Note any connections to the passages from Day 1.

Now read Romans 8:13.

> If you live according to the flesh you will die, but if by the Spirit you put to death the deeds of the body, you will live.

> **Question 4:** What are the two ways to live that are stated in this passage? What do you think Paul means practically by the second half of the verse?

Day 3—The War Against Bitterness

One of the most persistent and difficult sins to overcome is the sin of bitterness and an unforgiving spirit, especially when one has been wronged.

* **Question 5:** Describe a situation in which you have been embittered by the actions of another. What increased your bitterness? What strategies have you used to combat bitterness?

The sin of bitterness provides an opportunity to examine the interplay of past and future grace.

First study Ephesians 4:32 and Matthew 6:15.

Be kind to one another, tenderhearted, forgiving one another, as God in Christ forgave you.

But if you do not forgive others their trespasses, neither will your Father forgive your trespasses.

Question 6: How do these two passages motivate us to overcome bitterness and an unforgiving spirit?

Faith in God's forgiveness does not merely mean confidence that I am off the hook. It means confidence that this is the most precious thing in the world. That's why I use the word *cherish*. Saving faith cherishes being forgiven by God.

And there's the link with the battle against bitterness. You can go on holding a grudge if your faith simply means you are off the hook. But if faith means standing in awe of being forgiven by God, then you can't go on holding a grudge. You have fallen in love with mercy. It's your life. So you battle bitterness by fighting for the faith that stands in awe of God's forgiveness of your sins.[12]

Day 4—Bitterness and Future Grace

We have seen how past grace and fear of judgment can motivate us to resist bitterness. We now turn to see how future grace can further aid us in the fight against an unforgiving spirit.

Study 1 Peter 2:19–23.

[19]For this is a gracious thing, when, mindful of God, one endures sorrows while suffering unjustly. [20]For what credit is it if, when you sin and are beaten for it, you endure? But if when you do good and suffer for it you endure, this is a gracious thing in the sight of God. [21]For to this you have been called, because Christ also suffered for you, leaving you an example, so that you might follow in his steps. [22]He committed no sin, neither was deceit found in his mouth. [23]When he was reviled, he did not revile in return; when he suffered, he did not threaten, but continued entrusting himself to him who judges justly.

* **Question 7:** How did Jesus resist the temptation to hate and grow bitter at those who persecuted him? Underline key phrases. How do you know that Jesus is a model for us in this regard?

Look closely at Romans 12:19–21.

> [19]Beloved, never avenge yourselves, but leave it to the wrath of God, for it is written, "Vengeance is mine, I will repay," says the Lord." [20] To the contrary, "if your enemy is hungry, feed him; if he is thirsty, give him something to drink; for by so doing you will heap burning coals on his head." [21]Do not be overcome by evil, but overcome evil with good.

Question 8: According to this passage, what frees us from the need to avenge ourselves? What are we free to do instead of seek revenge?

DAY 5—LESSONS ON PATIENCE FROM THE STORY OF JOSEPH

The final sin that we will examine is the sin of impatience. To do so, we will reflect on the story of Joseph.

Read through the story of Joseph in your own Bible. It can be found in Genesis 37 and 39–50.

* **Question 9:** As you read the story of Joseph, note situations in which Joseph would be tempted to succumb to impatience. Are there any indications that Joseph does grow impatient in this passage?

Joseph is a remarkable example of perseverance in the midst of adversity and hardship. In a number of passages, he seems to mention the source of his remarkable patience.

Study Genesis 45:4–8 and Genesis 50:19–20.

[4]So Joseph said to his brothers, "Come near to me, please." And they came near. And he said, "I am your brother, Joseph, whom you sold into Egypt. [5]And now do not be distressed or angry with yourselves because you sold me here, for God sent me before you to preserve life. [6]For the famine has been in the land these two years, and there are yet five years in which there will be neither plowing nor harvest. [7]And God sent me before you to preserve for you a remnant on earth, and to keep alive for you many survivors. [8]So it was not you who sent me here, but God. He has made me a father to Pharaoh, and lord of all his house and ruler over all the land of Egypt.

[19]But Joseph said to them, "Do not fear, for am I in the place of God? [20]As for you, you meant evil against me, but God meant it for good, to bring it about that many people should be kept alive, as they are today."

Question 10: According to these passages, why was Joseph able to resist the temptation to impatience and hatred of his brothers? Underline the relevant phrases.

Further Up and Further In

Read "ANTHEM: Strategies for Fighting Lust," an online article at the Desiring God website.

Question 11: What does the acronym ANTHEM stand for? Which aspects of this strategy go beyond your normal strategies for fighting sexual sin?

Read or listen to "Practical Help for Praying for Help," an online sermon at the Desiring God website.

Question 12: What are the five steps that John Piper outlines to help us live the Christian life?

Read or listen to "The Present Power of a Future Possession," an online sermon at the Desiring God website.

Question 13: Identify the specific sufferings that the saints mentioned in Hebrews 10 choose to endure.

Question 14: What was their attitude as they endured the suffering? How were they able to endure such suffering with this kind of attitude?

Read the hymn "God Moves in a Mysterious Way" by William Cowper, as quoted in "Insanity and Spiritual Songs in the Soul of a Saint," an online conference message at the Desiring God website.

God moves in a mysterious way
His wonders to perform;
He plants his footsteps in the sea,
And rides upon the storm.

Deep in unfathomable mines
Of never failing skill,
He treasures up his bright designs
And works his sovereign will.

Ye fearful saints, fresh courage take,
The clouds ye so much dread
Are big with mercy, and shall break
In blessings on your head.

Judge not the lord by feeble sense,
But trust him for his grace;
behind a frowning providence
He hides a smiling face.

His purpose will ripen fast,
Unfolding every hour;
the bud may have a bitter taste,
But sweet will be the flower.

Blind unbelief is sure to err,
And scan his work in vain:
God is his own interpreter,
And he will make it plain.

Question 15: Record any reflections on the lyrics of this hymn that can help us to fight the sin of impatience.

→• *While You Watch the DVD, Take Notes* •←

Lust: Pursuing _____ _____ or
_____ in the mind with a view to
_____ _____ pleasures—with or
without _____ _____.

What is lust rooted in?

Be _____ lust or lust will be _____ you.

In the end there will be no _____ _____.
They will all be _____ _____, either
in the _____ or in _____.

What truths help us to resist impatience when we are forced to
walk the path of obedience in an unplanned place or at an
unplanned pace?

Final Summary of Living by Faith in Future Grace

_____ → _____ → _____ → _____

—➧ *After You Watch the DVD, Discuss What You've Learned* ✦—

1. What practical strategies did you learn to help wage war against sexual lust?

2. What practical strategies did you learn to help wage war against bitterness and an unforgiving spirit?

3. What practical strategies did you learn to help wage war against impatience?

—➧ *After You Discuss, Make Application* ✦—

1. What was the most meaningful part of this lesson for you? Was there a sentence, concept, or idea that really struck you? Why? Record your thoughts in the space below.

2. Choose one of the sins that have been discussed in the last two
    lessons and develop a customized strategy for fighting it in your
    own life. Be specific about ways that you will resist temptation
    and overcome this sin. Let an accountability partner know
    about your strategies.

REVIEW AND CONCLUSION

LESSON OBJECTIVES

It is our prayer that after you have finished this lesson…

- You will be able to summarize and synthesize what you've learned.
- You will hear what others in your group have learned.
- You will share with others how you have begun to live by faith in future grace.

WHAT HAVE YOU LEARNED?

There are no study questions to answer in preparation for this lesson. Instead, spend your time writing a few paragraphs that explain what you've learned in this group study. To help you do this, you may choose to review the notes you've taken in the previous lessons. Then, after you've written down what you've learned, write down some questions that still remain in your mind about anything addressed in these lessons. Be prepared to share these reflections and questions with the group in the next lesson. In particular, reflect on any other particular sins that weren't discussed and how you might begin to fight them by faith in future grace.

Notes

Use this space to record anything in the group discussion that you want
to remember.

LEADER'S GUIDE

As the leader of this group study, **it is imperative that you are completely familiar with this study guide** and with the *Future Grace* DVD Set. Therefore, it is our strong recommendation that you (1) read and understand the introduction, (2) skim each lesson, surveying its layout and content, and (3) read the entire Leader's Guide *before* you begin the group study and distribute the study guides. As you review this Leader's Guide, keep in mind that the material here is only a recommendation. As the leader of the study, feel free to adapt this study guide to your situation and context.

BEFORE LESSON 1
Before the first lesson, you will need to know approximately how many participants you will have in your group study. **Each participant will need his or her own study guide!** Therefore, be sure to order enough study guides. You will distribute these study guides at the beginning of the first lesson.

It is also our strong recommendation that you, as the leader, familiarize yourself with this study guide and the *Future Grace* DVD Set in order to answer any questions that might arise and also to ensure that each group session runs smoothly and maximizes the learning of the participants. It is not necessary for you to preview the *Future Grace* DVD in its entirety—although it certainly wouldn't hurt!—but you should be prepared to navigate your way through each DVD menu.

DURING LESSON 1
Each lesson is designed for a one-hour group session. Lessons 2–12 require preparatory work from the participant before this group session. Lesson 1, however, requires no preparation on the part of the participant.

The following schedule is how we suggest that you use the first hour of your group study:

Introduction to the Study Guide (5 minutes)
Introduce this study guide and the *Future Grace* DVD. Share with the group why you chose to lead the group study using these resources. Inform your group of the commitment that this study will require and motivate them to work hard. Pray for the twelve-week study, asking God for the grace you will need. Then distribute one study guide to each participant. You may read the introduction aloud, if you want, or you may immediately have the group turn to Lesson 1 (starting on page 5 of this study guide).

Personal Introductions (10 minutes)
Since group discussion will be an integral part of this guided study, it is crucial that each participant feels welcome and safe. The goal of each lesson is for every participant to contribute to the discussion in some way. Therefore, during these minutes, have participants each introduce themselves. You may choose to use the questions listed in the section titled "About Yourself," or you may ask questions of your own choosing.

DVD and Discussion (35 minutes)
Show the *Future Grace* DVD, Session 1, and have participants take notes in their study guides. Then proceed to the discussion questions, listed under the heading "After You Watch the DVD, Discuss What You've Learned."

Review and Closing (10 minutes)
End the group session by reviewing Lesson 2 with the group participants and informing them of the preparation that they must do before the group meets again. Encourage them to be faithful in preparing for the next lesson. Answer any questions that the group may have and then close in prayer.

BEFORE LESSONS 2–11

As the group leader, you should do all the preparation for each lesson that is required of the group participants, that is, the ten study questions. Furthermore, it is highly recommended that you complete the entire "Further Up and Further In" section. This is not required of the group participants, but it will enrich your preparation and help you to guide and shape the conversation more effectively.

The group leader should also preview the session of *Future Grace* that will be covered in the next lesson. So, for example, if the group participants are doing the preparatory work for Lesson 3, you should preview *Future Grace,* Session 3 before the group meets and views it. Previewing each session will better equip you to understand the material and answer questions. If you want to pause the DVD in the midst of the session in order to clarify or discuss, previewing the session will allow you to plan where you want to take your pauses.

Finally, you may want to supplement or modify the discussion questions or the application assignment. Please remember that **this study guide is a resource**; any additions or changes you make that better match the study to your particular group are encouraged. As the group leader, your own discernment, creativity, and guidance are invaluable, and you should adapt the material as you see fit.

**Plan for about two hours of your own preparation
before each lesson!**

DURING LESSONS 2–11

Again, let us stress that during Lessons 2–11, you may use the group time in whatever way you desire. The following schedule, however, is what we suggest:

Discussion (15 minutes)

Begin your time with prayer. The tone you set in your prayer will likely be impressed upon the group participants: if your prayer is serious and heartfelt, the group participants will be serious about prayer; if your prayer is hasty, sloppy, or a token gesture, the group participants will share this same attitude toward prayer. So model the kind of praying that you desire your students to imitate. Remember, the blood of Jesus has bought your access to the throne of grace.

After praying, review the preparatory work that the participants completed. How did they answer the questions? Which questions did they find to be the most interesting or the most confusing? What observations or insights can they share with the group? If you would like to review some tips for leading productive discussion, please turn to Appendix B at the end of this study guide.

The group participants will be provided an opportunity to apply what they've learned in Lessons 2–11. As the group leader, you can choose whether it would be appropriate for the group to discuss these assignments during this fifteen-minute time slot.

DVD Viewing (25 minutes)[13]

Play the session for *Future Grace* that corresponds to the lesson you're studying. You may choose to pause the DVD at crucial points to check for understanding and provide clarification. Or, you may choose to watch the DVD without interruption.

Discussion and Closing (20 minutes)

Foster discussion on what was taught during John Piper's session. You may do this by first reviewing the DVD notes (under the heading "While You Watch the DVD, Take Notes") and then proceeding to the discussion questions, listed under the heading "After You Watch the DVD, Discuss What You've Learned." These discussion questions are meant to be springboards that launch the group into further and deeper discussion. Don't feel constrained to these questions if the group discussion begins to move in other helpful directions.

Close the time by briefly reviewing the application section and the homework that is expected for the next lesson. Pray and dismiss.

BEFORE LESSON 12

It is important that you encourage the group participants to complete the preparatory work for Lesson 12. This assignment invites the participants to reflect on what they've learned and what remaining questions they still have. As the group leader, this would be a helpful assignment for you to complete as well. In addition, you may want to write down the key concepts of this DVD series that you want the group participants to walk away with.

DURING LESSON 12

The group participants are expected to complete a reflection exercise as part of their preparation for Lesson 12. The bulk of the group time during this last lesson should be focused on reviewing and synthesizing what was learned. Encourage each participant to share some of his or her recorded thoughts. Attempt to answer any remaining questions that they might have.

To close this last lesson, you might want to spend extended time in prayer. If appropriate, take prayer requests relating to what the participants have learned in these twelve lessons, and bring these requests to God.

It would be completely appropriate for you, the group leader, to give a final charge or word of exhortation to end this group study. Speak from your heart and out of the overflow of joy that you have in God.

Please receive our blessing for all you group leaders who choose to use this study guide:

> *The LORD bless you and keep you; the LORD make his*
> *face to shine upon you and be gracious to you; the LORD*
> *lift up his countenance upon you and give you peace.*
> *(Numbers 6:24–26)*

SIX-SESSION INTENSIVE OPTION

We understand that there are circumstances which may prohibit a group from devoting twelve sessions to this study. In view of this, we have designed a six-session intensive option for groups that need to complete the material in less time. In the intensive option, the group should meet for two hours each week. Here is our suggestion for how to complete the material in six weeks:

Week 1   Introduction to this Study Guide and Lesson 1
          (DVD Session 1)
Week 2   Lessons 2 and 3 (DVD Sessions 2 and 3)
Week 3   Lessons 4 and 5 (DVD Sessions 4 and 5)
Week 4   Lessons 6 and 7 (DVD Sessions 6 and 7)
Week 5   Lessons 8 and 9 (DVD Sessions 8 and 9)
Week 6   Lessons 10 and 11 (DVD Sessions 10 and 11)

Notice that we have not included Lesson 12 in the intensive option. Moreover, because each participant is required to complete two lessons per week, it will be necessary to combine the number of "days" within each lesson so that all of the material is covered. Thus, for example, during Week 2 in the intensive option, each participant will complete:

- Lesson 2, Days 1 and 2, on the first day;
- Lesson 2, Days 3 and 4, on the second day;
- Lesson 2, Day 5 and Lesson 3, Day 1, on the third day;

- Lesson 3, Days 2 and 3, on the fourth day;
- Lesson 3, Days 4 and 5, on the fifth day.

Because of the amount of material, we recommend that students focus on questions marked with an asterisk (*) first, and then, if time permits, complete the rest of the questions.

LEADING PRODUCTIVE DISCUSSIONS

Note: This material has been adapted from curricula produced by Bethlehem Press, a ministry of Bethlehem College and Seminary. It is used by permission.

I t is our conviction that the best group leaders foster an environment in their group which engages the participants. Most people learn by solving problems or by working through things that provoke curiosity or concern. Therefore, we discourage you from ever lecturing for the entire lesson. Although a group leader will constantly shape conversation, clarifying and correcting as needed, he or she will probably not talk for the majority of the lesson. This study guide is meant to facilitate an investigation into biblical truth—an investigation that is shared by the group leader and the participants. Therefore, we encourage you to adopt the posture of a fellow-learner who invites participation from everyone in the group.

It might surprise you how eager people can be to share what they have learned in preparing for each lesson. Therefore, you should invite participation by asking your group participants to share their discoveries. Here are some of our "tips" on facilitating discussion that is engaging and helpful:

- Don't be uncomfortable with silence initially. Once the first participant shares his or her response, others will be likely to join in. But if you cut the silence short by prompting them,

then they are more likely to wait for you to prompt them
every time.

- Affirm every answer, if possible, and draw out the participants by asking for clarification. Your aim is to make them
feel comfortable sharing their ideas and learning, so be
extremely hesitant to shut down a group member's contribu-
tion or trump it with your own. This does not mean,
however, that you shouldn't correct false ideas—just do it in
a spirit of gentleness and love.

- Don't allow a single person, or group of persons, to domi-
nate the discussion. Involve everyone, if possible, and
intentionally invite participation from those who are more
reserved or hesitant.

- Labor to show the significance of their study. Emphasize the
things that the participants could not have learned without
doing the homework.

- Avoid talking too much. The group leader should not
monopolize the discussion, but rather guide and shape it.
If the group leader does the majority of the talking, the
participants will be less likely to interact and engage, and
therefore they will not learn as much. Avoid constantly
adding the definitive last word.

- The group leader should feel the freedom to linger on a topic
or question if the group demonstrates interest. The group
leader should also pursue digressions that are helpful and
relevant. There is a balance to this, however: the group
leader *should* attempt to cover the material. So avoid the
extreme of constantly wandering off topic, but also avoid
the extreme of limiting the conversation in a way that
squelches curiosity or learning.

- The group leader's passion, or lack of it, is infectious.
Therefore, if you demonstrate little enthusiasm for the
material, it is almost inevitable that your participants will
likewise be bored. But if you have a genuine excitement for

what you are studying, and if you truly think Bible study is worthwhile, then your group will be impacted positively. Therefore, it is our recommendation that before you come to the group, you spend enough time working through the homework and praying, so that you can overflow with genuine enthusiasm for the Bible and for God in your group. This point cannot be stressed enough. Delight yourself in God and in his Word!

NOTES

1. While this study guide is ideally suited for a twelve-session study, it is possible to complete it in six sessions. For instructions on how to use this study guide for a six-session group study, turn to Appendix A: Six-Session Intensive Option.

2. Although this resource is designed to be used in a group setting, it can also be used by the independent learner. Such a learner would have to decide for himself how to use this resource in the most beneficial way. We would suggest doing everything but the group discussion, if possible.

3. Twenty-five minutes is only an approximation. Some sessions are longer; others are shorter.

4. John Piper, "Let Your Passion Be Single," an online conference message at the Desiring God website, www.desiringgod.org.

5. John Piper, "Preaching Practical Holiness," an online sermon at the Desiring God website.

6. John Piper, "Obedience Confirms Our Standing with God," an online sermon at the Desiring God website.

7. We will only look at three of these four reasons here. The final reason we will examine in Lesson 6.

8. John Piper, "How to Kill Sin, Part 3," an online sermon at the Desiring God website.

9. John Piper, "Jesus Is Alive to Serve," an online sermon at the Desiring God website.

10. John Piper, "Christian Hedonism: Forgive the Label, but Don't Miss the Truth," an online article at the Desiring God website.

11. John Piper, "Today's Mercies for Today's Troubles," an online sermon at the Desiring God website.

12. John Piper, "Battling the Unbelief of Bitterness," an online sermon at the Desiring God website.

13. Twenty-five minutes is only an approximation. Some of the sessions are shorter, while some are longer. You may need to budget your group time differently, depending upon which session you are viewing.

LIVE IN THE FREEDOM
OF FUTURE GRACE

John Piper's foundational and biblical exploration of the
power of grace over the patterns of sin guides readers
through thirty days of reflection to freedom.

Find more information about this book,
as well as the *Future Grace DVD*, on
WaterBrookMultnomah.com!

EXPERIENCE THE LIFELONG PLEASURES OF KNOWING GOD.

This updated edition of *Desiring God* now includes a study guide that facilitates discussion of this classic work on Christian hedonism in small group settings.

Also Available:
Desiring God DVD
Desiring God DVD Study Guide

John Piper navigates the biblical evidence to help us see and savor what the pleasures of God show us about Him, so that we might become like the One we behold. This updated edition includes a study guide for small group or individual use.

Also Available:
The Pleasures of God DVD
The Pleasures of God DVD Study Guide